Income Distribution
in Jordan

Published in cooperation with the
Friedrich Ebert Stiftung

Income Distribution in Jordan

EDITED BY

Kamel Abu Jaber, Matthes Buhbe, and Mohammad Smadi

Westview Press

BOULDER, SAN FRANCISCO, & OXFORD

Westview Special Studies on the Middle East

Copyright © 1990 by Friedrich Ebert Stiftung

Published in 1990 in the United States of America by Westview Press, Inc., 5500 Central Avenue, Boulder, Colorado 80301, and in the United Kingdom by Westview Press, Inc., 36 Lonsdale Road, Summertown, Oxford OX2 7EW

Library of Congress Cataloging-in-Publication Data
Income distribution in Jordan/edited by Kamel Abu Jaber, Matthes
     Buhbe, and Mohammad Smadi.
          p.   cm.--(Westview special studies on the Middle East)
     ISBN 0-8133-7933-4
     1. Income distribution--Jordan.   2. Income distribution--West
Bank.   3. Income distribution--Gaza Strip.   I. Abu Jaber, Kamel,
1932-   . II. Buhbe, Matthes, 1949-   . III. Smadi, Mohammad, 1950-
IV. Series.
HC415.26.Z9I53   1990
339.2'095695--dc20   89-48382
                                                                                     CIP

Camera-ready production by Al Kutba, Publishers, Amman, Jordan
Printed and bound in the United States of America

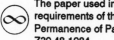

10   9   8   7   6   5   4   3   2   1

Contents

PART THREE
POLICY ISSUES

Acknowledgments

This book was made possible through the support and effort of several individuals and institutions. The editors first wish to express their indebtedness to His Royal Highness Crown Prince Al-Hassan Bin Talal, whose interest and active support were vital to the completion of this publication. We particularly appreciate his efforts to involve Jordanians from all walks of life in the discussion of issues of social justice such as those contained in this book.

Special thanks also go to Dr. Jawad Al-Anani, former president of the Royal Scientific Society, and his staff; to Dr. Taher Kana'an, former minister of planning, and his staff; and to Dr. Fawwaz Tuqan, former minister of social development.

Finally, we are especially grateful to the Friedrich Ebert Foundation for its moral and financial support of the production of this publication.

Kamel Abu Jaber
Matthes Buhbe
Mohammad Smadi

Introduction

Jordan's economy has witnessed tremendous growth since the early 1960s. This growth and development came as the result of several factors, the chief catalyst for which was the steady hand of the leadership at the top coupled with a rather liberal sociopolitical and economic atmosphere. This gave the country a measure of stability that allowed for healthy progress. In the second half of the 1980s, Jordan had to face economic recession and problems of public debt finance. However, the Jordanian experiment in socioeconomic development still contrasts favorably to more rigid ideological models elsewhere in the area.

Rational and eclectic, the Jordanian experiment continues to avoid extremes in all aspects of life. Such an approach has been conducive to the growth of a viable partnership between the private and the public sectors. During the past few decades, the public sector has engaged in projects that the private sector could not undertake because of an inadequate rate of return, the scale of the intended enterprise, or the long duration necessary for profits to accrue. Sometimes the private sector, recognizably small in any case in the country, just simply could not mobilize the needed resources, either human or financial.

To a large extent it was the realization that economic inequality would inevitably lead to social cleavage, discontent, and eventually to instability and violence that lay, at least in part, behind Jordan's development effort. Socioeconomic development aspires not only to the achievement of social peace but also to a more equitable income distribution. These issues became more immediate following the 1948 Arab-Israeli War and the consequent establishment of the state of Israel, which resulted in the first mass exodus of Palestinian refugees into Jordan. The refugees brought with them new skills and talents; they also exerted a considerable amount of pressure on the host country to meet developmental challenges. Since then the pressure for change and development has been internalized, although external influences also remain. The changes that have occurred have been, on the whole, impressive, although by no means even. Differences, some apparent and glaring, remain and can be seen in the dissimilarities between urban and rural areas and among sections of the major cities. New classes or groups have arisen, including an expanding middle class of professionals, doctors, lawyers, engineers, educators;

the modern laboring class; and the mostly mercantile business community.

Planning for change became an accepted concept in Jordan right at the beginning of the 1950s. By the 1960s, socioeconomic plans had become welcome tools for the mobilization of resources. Each successive socioeconomic plan delineated goals to be pursued during the next period. The basic infrastructure necessary for development continues to be the responsibility of the government. Education, health care and welfare services have witnessed considerable advances. Transportation, communications, and other services have kept in step with developments in other sectors of the economy.

Along with the changes witnessed in the physical aspects of the landscape itself came changes in lifestyles, jobs, social behavior, and even values. This growth has affected all aspects of life to such an extent that the Jordan of today bears little resemblance to the Jordan of yesterday.

It is within this frame of reference that the following chapters raise questions on sensitive issues related to the concept of social justice and the equitable distribution of the benefits of development. The asking of such questions is necessary if only to evaluate the present stage of development, to take stock of what has already occurred, and perhaps to better plan future activities.

Not only has Jordan itself changed; the planning process has also undergone significant changes. During the last quarter of 1988, a number of regional planning conferences was held at the initiative of H.R.H. Crown Prince Al-Hassan Bin Talal to involve the grass roots of Jordanian society in the planning process. People from all walks of life--ordinary citizens, local government officials, academics, and tribal chiefs--were invited to participate in these conferences so that previously uninvolved sectors of society could take part in the process of socioeconomic planning. Under the enlightened leadership of the crown prince, socioeconomic planning is shifting its emphasis in order to involve input from the lower level. The popular response has been enthusiastic and has been seen as a step in the right direction, incorporating as it does the philosophy that local input can definitely enhance as well as enrich the entire development process.

That there may be unevenness or that there are difficulties goes without saying. Such rapid development as has occurred in Jordan in such a short space of time is bound to have some negative results. The overall picture, however, is a healthy one. Given time, and particularly if a peaceful settlement of the Palestinian-Israeli conflict is reached, the country will surely achieve self-sufficiency and prosperity.

This book is not a comprehensive study: There are only ten short chapters on distributional aspects of economic and social development. A number of professional Jordanian economists was asked to contribute in a joint effort to shed light on a field of research that had hitherto been neglected in Jordan.

While Jordanian decisionmakers were investing great care in various aspects of development, as can be witnessed in the plan documents for 1976-1980, 1981-1985, and 1986-1990 on economic and social development, they were also coping with rapid socioeconomic change. Therefore, it seems useful, indeed imperative, to establish a scientific platform as a preliminary study for the distributional aspects of this development.

The contributions to this book are only a first step in this direction. By presenting them to a broader audience, we hope to achieve three objectives:

To enrich the knowledge on economic conditions in Jordan beyond simple indicators such as per capita income.

To establish an improved platform for the economic analysis of income distribution in Jordan and to demonstrate how useful this can be for planners and decisionmakers.

To give incentives for more detailed and deeper studies still to come.

Part One of the book addresses the relationship between economic development and income distribution. In Chapter 1, the minister of planning, Taher Kana'an, focuses on the social dimension of economic change. He presents the main ideas behind the various development plans of Jordan since the 1960s and also describes some of the achievements made in education, health, and other public services as well as the role of income distribution in this context.

In Chapter 2, Adeeb Haddad reviews the statistical evidence on distribution and economic development in Jordan: functional income distribution, size income distribution, household expenditure distribution, and the issue of poverty, including policies and measures taken with a view to poverty eradication.

In Chapter 3, Fayez Tarawneh chooses a theoretical approach of great practical importance in his attempt to model the determinants of inequality in economic development. He presents a system of sixteen simultaneous equations to show the influence of key variables of development on the level of distributional inequality. If applied to Jordan, the results could be weighed against the Kuznets hypothesis. According to Kuznets, economic growth in developing countries initially creates an increase in distributional inequality, which is followed by a reduction in inequality. An application of Tarawneh's model to Jordan would allow both another test for this hypothesis and a study of those factors that determine distributional inequality of income in Jordan.

Part Two deals with the economics of wage and income distribution in an empirical manner. The authors make extensive use of data that have not been available until recently. In Chapter 4, Radwan Sha'ban uses the preliminary results of an income and expenditure household survey carried out in 1986. He calculates inequality measures such as the Gini coefficient for 1986 and compares his findings with data for 1973 and 1980. In contrast with 1973 and 1986, 1980 fell right in the middle of an economic boom, so Sha'ban addresses the question of whether the benefits and losses of boom and recession in Jordan are evenly distributed across the different population groups. According to Sha'ban, inequality was greater in the boom year 1980 than in either 1973 or 1986. Sha'ban also extends his analysis to the interregional distribution of income. During the period 1973-1986, there was a less unequal distribution in the rural areas than in the urban areas. But the inequality gap has become considerably smaller over time.

In Chapter 5, Saleh Al-Khasawneh analyzes wage differentials in all branches of the private sector. He was able to obtain a data set for 1987 from the Social Security Corporation that covered about 95 percent of the workers in the private sector, both Jordanian and non-Jordanian. Al-Khasawneh uses this information to calculate monthly average wages and compares them across variables such as profession, sex, geographic area, age, social status, and nationality. For example, he finds the average wage to be higher for Jordanians than for non-Jordanians and for males than for females in almost all branches; in contrast, the average wage for non-Jordanian females is higher than that for Jordanian females. Al-Khasawneh also explains the factors that might create such wage differentials.

Ahmad Malkawi, in Chapter 6, studies the different wage levels of male and female workers in establishments hiring five persons or more for the period 1980-1986. He concentrates on two aspects. First, he divides the workers into university graduates and non graduates. Second, he groups the workers by eight major economic activities. He further considers the effect of the size of an establishment on wage differentiation. Like Saleh Al-Khasawneh, Malkawi finds higher wages for males than for females. He also finds that sex/wage differentials have not narrowed with Jordan's economic growth during the years and that sex/wage differentials are greater for university graduates independent of the size of the establishment employing them.

Chapter 7 is based on a study completed in December 1987 by Abdelfattah Abu Shokor of An-Najah National University, Nablus. He tackles the following areas: pattern of personal income distribution in the occupied territories, degree of inequality according to the Gini coefficient, regional aspects of income distribution, and causes and social impact of inequality.

Part Three deals with distributional issues as these are linked to social policy in Jordan. Mohammad Al-Saqour, in Chapter 8, studies the problem of definition and measurement of poverty in Jordan. He defines destitution, absolute poverty, and relative poverty and constructs an absolute poverty line in Jordan. He also discusses the four major Jordanian institutions that deal with the assistance of the poor.

Chapter 9 relates Jordan's social security scheme to macroeconomic development, particularly income distribution. Using his detailed knowledge of social security regulations, the size and characteristics of membership, the scheme, and other available data of the Social Security Corporation, Ghassan Musallam analyzes the inflow and outflow of funds. He then suggests some steps toward redistribution, as embodied in the concept of a social budget of the nation, and a wages policy.

Chapter 10 focuses on Jordan's health care supply, both by public and private institutions. Abed Kharabsheh also describes the personal health care expenditure of various income groups and links the private demand for health services to the level of income.

The book concludes with an appendix that gives some general facts concerning Jordan's economy and income distribution in order to guide the less specialized reader through the high concentration of data included in the body of the text.

We hope this first step toward a thorough analysis of income distribution in Jordan will encourage further research efforts in the near future.

PART ONE

Income Distribution
and Economic Development

1

Observations on the Social Dimension in Jordan's Approach to Development

Taher H. Kana'an

1. Concepts of Development Planning in Jordan

The first two decades of the development of the Hashemite Kingdom of Jordan, the 1950s and 1960s, coincided with what has internationally come to be considered the first generation of thinking in the economics and philosophy of development. That philosophy, and the development programs that grew from it in many countries including Jordan, especially those programs that were undertaken under World Bank guidance or participation, were characterized in particular by an almost exclusive drive for and emphasis on the realization of rates of growth of gross national product (GNP) higher than the demographic rates of growth of the population. The base indicator of development for this philosophy was the rate of growth in average per capita income.

Yet by the early 1970s, the second generation of thinking in development economics brought development theory to a new phase in which objectives were expanded significantly to include far more than growth in GNP. It had become apparent that even when high rates of overall growth in the national product were achieved, this often disguised the persistence of a substantial, even at times growing, segment of the population below the absolute poverty line. Such rates of growth were also often accompanied by rising unemployment and unequal distribution of the benefits of development among the various groups and strata of society.

Hence, the second generation of development theorists began to look well beyond the aggregates of national income and to analyze its detailed component factors and the interrelationships through which these affect the basic needs of the majority of the populace. Concern began to center on the factors and components that affected the forms of poverty, its causes, its endemic centers, and the reasons for which such poverty persisted and even increased. The severe disadvantages that affected a wide mass of the population, such as malnutrition, disease, illiteracy, subhuman housing conditions, and the spread of unemployment, came to the forefront. Thus, the attitude toward development evolved from one in which development was an end in itself to one in which development was a means of fulfilling basic needs and overcoming the problems that stood in the way of effecting a genuine and comprehensive change in the nature and quality of Jordanian economic and social life. Improving the standards of health care, education, and civic amenities of the large majority of citizenry and narrowing the disparities that separated the different strata and social groups in the various regions of the country became priority targets.

The early programs of the Jordan Development Board centered on achieving aggregate growth and investing in the physical infrastructure. The social benefits of such programs were taken for granted. We find, for instance, that the main objectives of the Seven-Year Program (1964-1970) were to reduce the deficit in the balance of trade and to reduce budgetary dependence on foreign aid. Two further goals were to raise average per capita income--irrespective of its distribution--and to reduce the rate of unemployment. In order to achieve a reduction of budgetary dependence on foreign aid, the program specified that it was necessary to increase government revenue by means of higher taxes. When the choices of the instruments and means of implementation of this increase were being determined, the planners sought "to be as equitable as possible" requiring that taxes be imposed on luxury goods, capital gains, inheritances, and bequests. Yet considerations of social justice did not prevent the imposition of taxes that were "regressive and inequitable" when these promised to "provide needed revenue to cover the growing decline in budget support."

The 1970s, however, brought a major qualitative advance in the main approach to development. For the Three-Year Plan (1973-1975), the following primary objective was chosen: "To realize the highest possible level of economic activity and employment, and to develop manpower skills, qualifications, and capabilities in the service of development." The second objective was to "realize the highest possible rate of growth of GNP," and the third objective was "the useful distribution of public services and the benefits of development among all regions of the Kingdom and all groups and strata of society." The Three-Year Plan also showed great concern with the human dimension when it concluded that "development becomes meaningful with the realization of popular participation in political and social life, and when the individual citizen recognizes that he has a positive role to play in the implementation of development and definite rights to the more comprehensive and fair distribution of the wealth and benefits thereby created."

The Jordanian economy entered a new stage in the 1970s that was distinguished from preceding phases by a degree of economic affluence. The consequences of the great rise in oil prices, the increase in the revenues of the oil producing countries, and the expanded investment and employment capabilities of these countries were reflected positively in levels of economic activity in Jordan. Emigration of Jordanian skilled labor to countries of the Arabian Gulf rose sharply from 153,000 in 1973 to 198,000 in 1975. The remittances of this émigré work force grew substantially, as did direct aid from these countries to the Jordanian Treasury. In less than two years, the nature of the economic problems of the country was transformed. Unemployment dropped from its early 1970s level of 14% to substantially lower levels, and as external resources that were once scare became available, the realization of optimal growth in the production of goods and commodities replaced the development of labor skills as the first priority of Jordanian planning. Thus, the prime objective of the First Five-Year Plan (1975-1980) was "to bring about a fundamental change in the economic infrastructure through the development of the manufacturing sector." The second objective was the "realization of high real rates of growth." The goals of fair distribution of income and labor development were relegated to third and fourth positions, respectively. Hence, social justice ceased to be viewed as an end in itself and became a constraint, the achievement of which was conditional on the realization of the other main goals. The planners' concern in conceptualizing their national and sectoral plans was thus limited to preventing any of their strategies and policies from exercising any negative effects on social justice.

The degree to which Jordanian planners have been influenced by the evolution of international development thought became more apparent in the Second Five-Year Plan (1981-1985), which unequivocally stated in its first intellectual premise that "man has always been at the heart of all successive Jordanian Plans. It is imperative that all sectors and capabilities of the Jordanian Economy be directed in the service of Man, the development of society and its well being." The objectives were to include, for the first time, "the provision of all basic needs and services, especially water, housing, health, education and transportation" in addition to "limiting disparities in the levels of income" and "narrowing disparities among the various regions of the country."

2. Achievements in Social Development

As for the achievements realized within this context, the following may be considered noteworthy.

2.1 Education

All successive Jordanian development plans have consistently sought to expand the educational base to include all groups of society and all regions of the country (urban, rural, and desert). To achieve this goal, the first nine years of compulsory education were made free. Enrollment in elementary education for the relevant age group rose from 77% in 1960 to 99% in 1986, one of the highest rates in the world. This increase resulted in a reduction in the level of illiteracy, which by 1987 was 26%. Four universities have been established in different regions of the country to spread higher education beyond the confines of the capital. Financial support has been extended to institutions of higher education to reduce the costs of tertiary education and make it more accessible to all social strata, so that the financial contribution of a university student toward his or her education will not exceed half the real costs. The end result of these policies has been to expand the range of opportunities available to greater numbers of the upcoming generation and thereby significantly to improve and diversify the skills and qualifications they could offer in the market-place, whether within Jordan or abroad. Needless to say, this achievement was directly reflected in the level of income and standards of living of most of the population.

2.2 Health

Great consideration was given by the development plans to the provision of health services to all citizens in all parts of the kingdom through the systematic establishment of government hospitals and infirmaries. The number of physicians of all specializations rose from less than 3 per 10,000 in 1961 to 11.4 per 10,000 in 1985. It is worthwhile to note that the average number of physicians per 10,000 for all middle income developing countries does not exceed 2.1. The number of hospital beds also rose to 19 per 10,000. The most advanced medical equipment and machinery were installed in hospitals and infirmaries across the country, and large numbers of paramedical and technical staff were trained.

The government has also been concerned with the vital area of public health, which most directly meets the health needs of the less fortunate strata of society. To this end comprehensive public health awareness campaigns were carried out throughout the country. The success of these campaigns was attested to by the significant drop in the infant mortality rate (from 151 per 1,000 live births in 1961 to 41 per 1,000 live births in 1987) and the near disappearance of such epidemic diseases as tuberculosis and malaria.

2.3 Housing

Another priority of successive Jordanian plans has been the provision of housing to middle and low income groups through the Housing Corporation and the Urban Development Corporation. The principle of fair geographic distribution of housing projects among the various regions of the country was observed as far as possible, and a specialized housing bank was created to raise the finance necessary for these schemes to continue and expand.

2.4 Electricity and Water

The provision of basic public infrastructural services to the population at large in even the remotest of regions has been an ongoing, major concern. The electricity and water supply networks were expanded and by 1988 directly reached more than 95% of the population. Pricing these services was carried out in such a way as to place them within the means of the various social groups. The rates paid for units of electricity consumed were modified in 1984 to distinguish among the various social beneficiary groups on the assumption that the level of consumption correlated directly with the level of income and standard of living. A "high consumption" kilowatt/hour of electricity was thus priced at about 160% of its "low consumption" counterpart. A similar scale was adopted in the pricing of drinking water; differences in the levels of income and geographic locations of the various user groups were taken into consideration. Thus, the rates large users were charged could be up to four times as high as the rates charged low consumption users, and the rates charged outside the capital, Amman, were set at about 80% of the rate charged high consumption Ammanis and less than 66% of the rate paid by low consumption Ammanis.

2.5 Popular Participation

The networks of basic services that have been provided in education, health, training and labor development, and other important areas of development have aimed at promoting a better prepared and more productive individual--one who is able to take charge of his or her own resources, improve his or her standard of living, and contribute to the evolution of economic and social decisions. To fulfill this goal, in the early 1980s the planning process began to invite and encourage popular participation in the drawing up of development plans. This trend was reinforced when preparations for the Third Five-Year Plan (1986-1990) were initiated. In addition to Sectoral Committees, Development Councils were formed in all eight governorates. Each council drew up its own regional development plan in conjunction and interaction with the national plan and the sectoral plans. The role of the Development Councils was further strengthened in the implementation stage as they were invited to participate in the process of follow-up and adjustment during the two subsequent years.

2.6 Distribution of Income

The development plans did not seek to specifically affect the distribution of income. Thus, income distribution policies have remained mostly implicit; they have a direct bearing only on the choice of means and for reaching the primary economic objective. For although planners have always recognized that there were differences in the economic and social conditions enjoyed by different sectors of the community, development plans have generally addressed macroeconomic problems without directly tackling standards of living or levels of economic benefits and their distribution among individuals. To the limited extent to which distribution was practiced, it was carried out indirectly by means of higher customs duties on luxury goods and exemptions of those basic and staple goods and commodities whose provision and prices affected the standards of living of all. The government has also adopted a progressive income tax policy and structure, although the implementation of this continues to be problematical. Taxes are collected efficiently and comprehensively from the civil service, government employees, and low income groups, but there is a high incidence of tax evasion among private companies and corporations, which are normally owned by the better off social groups.

Monetary policy was also characterized by a conservative approach that acted to restrain the widening of disparities among the various social strata and groups. This was effected by keeping the general level of prices and monetary inflation under control. Although some development plans did suggest the imposition of taxes on wealth and on capital gains, these suggestions did not meet with sufficient support to become policy. As a consequence of this neutral approach, levels of fairness in distribution of wealth fluctuated with the fluctuation in the economy. Even though average per capita income doubled several times in the aftermath of the first oil-price revolution in the 1970s, the disparities among the various income groups widened for the same period (1973-1980) (see Chapter 4). Income distribution did change toward greater fairness in the period 1980-1986, which was characterized by a slowing down of the economy.

3. Future Prospects

The primary shift in Jordanian development planning away from the previous emphasis on production to an emphasis on the distribution of the economic benefits of development to all social groups and national regions and the accompanying shift away from investment in the physical infrastructure to investment in human resources are final and irrevocable. They constitute a qualitative transformation of policy that will only be heightened and reinforced over time. The motivation behind this new orientation is by no means limited to intellectual enlightenment as to the true meaning of development and the centrality of human beings to it; the motivation is also related to practical considerations linked with changes in the volume, growth, and composition of Jordanian labor on the one hand, and changes in the makeup of the regional market and the roles of Jordanian production and labor in it, on the other.

Jordanian labor will be characterized in the 1990s by a high rate of growth in line with the high rate of population growth and the predominance of young people in the demographic structure. It is estimated that no fewer than fifty thousand persons will enter the labor market every year during the 1990s. These new entrants will generally have completed the ten years of compulsory education as a minimum and will include a vast number of university graduates. Meanwhile, the ability of the traditional regional market to absorb the labor force has been severely curtailed. This will force to a position of top priority and concern planning for the absorption of a highly qualified work force and for the transformation of the overall production structure to accommodate this work force and create productive job opportunities for it. It will also be imperative to transform the educational and training infrastructure so that it can adapt to the expected changes in the infrastructures of production in local and regional markets.

This will necessitate the creation of a comprehensive and highly detailed base of labor information that specifies the composition of the expected supply of labor, its levels and types of educational and professional qualifications, and the expected demand for labor in the local and regional markets. Moreover, in these circumstances the process of public participation in planning will undoubtedly reflect growing concern with the equitable distribution of the benefits of development among all social groups and national regions.

In addition to the previously described shift away from the macroaggregates of production and national income to their component factors and details, a parallel shift has occurred away from investment in material capital to investment in human capital, which takes the form of developing human capabilities and qualifications. This investment is based on the view that the individual is the driving "engine" of development and at the same time is the ultimate objective of the development process. Thus, Jordan's development plans and programs and development theory are well attuned to the evolution of thought in development economics.

Bibliography

Chenery, H.B.: "The Structural Approach to Development Policy." *American Economic Review* 65 (1975), pp. 310-316.

Hirschman, A.O.: *The Strategy of Economic Development.* New Haven, Conn.: Yale University Press, 1958.

Jordan Development Board: *Seven Year Program for Economic Development, 1964-1970.* Amman, 1965.

Lewis, W.A.: *The Theory of Economic Growth.* Homewood, Ill.: Irwin, 1955.

Little, I.M.D.: *Economic Development--Theory, Policy and International Relations.* New York: Basic Books, 1982.

Ministry of Planning: *Five Year Plan for Economic and Social Development, 1981-1985.* Amman, 1981.

_____: *Five Year Plan for Economic and Social Development, 1986-1990.* Amman, 1986.

National Planning Council: *Three Year Development Plan, 1973-1975.* Amman, 1972.

_____: *Five Year Development Plan, 1976-1980.* Amman, 1976.

United Nations Children's Fund/Ministry of Health: *Situation Analysis: Children and Women in the Hashemite Kingdom of Jordan.* Amman, 1989, unpublished.

2

Jordan's Income Distribution in Retrospect

Adeeb Haddad

1. Introduction

In the mid-1950s and early 1960s, economists and planners did not consider the distribution of income in developing countries to be a major policy problem. The prevailing view was that rapid economic growth would lead naturally to improved conditions for everyone. More recently, the issue of income distribution has become the most debated issue in the field of economic development due to its direct link to the concept of equity and growth.

Jordan recognizes the vital importance of an equitable distribution of the country's resources both among individuals and across the various regions of the kingdom. To this end, more recent social and economic development plans collectively emphasize the vital importance of reducing the disparities in income levels among the various sectors of the population and of achieving a more equitable distribution of gross national product (GNP) and the benefits of economic development.

Although inhibited by a lack of adequate, up-to-date information, this chapter will nevertheless attempt to capture the nature and context of income distribution and poverty in Jordan. The chapter is divided into six parts. The first is this introduction. The second part outlines developments in wages and the operating surplus based on the records of national income accounts. The third part deals with the distribution of different levels of income in urban and rural areas. The fourth focuses on expenditure distribution by family and individual. The fifth part examines factors contributing to inequality of income distribution. The sixth part highlights the concept of poverty in Jordan. The chapter concludes with a summary of arguments and a discussion of recommendations.

2. Developments in Wages and the Operating Surplus

There are two methods of measuring national income in Jordan. The first consists in measuring production through expenditure, which includes consumption, investment, government expenditure, and exports minus imports. The second method of measuring national income consists in adding up the returns of the factors of production. Factors of production comprise labor and capital (including land). Thus, the returns of the factors of production consist of labor income--wages and salaries, including self-employment income--and capital income--dividends, profit, interest, and rent. Theoretically, both methods should give the same result because they represent two sides of the same coin. For the purpose of analysis, developments in wages and salaries and capital income (operating surplus) are grouped into three distinct periods.

2.1 First Period (1952-1966)

During this period, wages and salaries increased in nominal terms from JD 13.7 million in 1952 to JD 57.5 million in 1966, with an annual average growth rate of 10.8%. This was mainly attributed to an increase in the size of the labor force accompanied by an increase in average individual wages. The operating surplus witnessed an annual average growth rate of only 7.5%, rising from JD 30.8 million in 1952 to JD 58.0 million in 1966. Thus, gross domestic product (GDP) increased from JD 50.5 million in 1952 to JD 170.6 million in 1966.

This period was characterized by a relative stability of general prices. The price index for 1966 was 122.7 points, an increase of 22.7 points from the base year of 1952. Thus, the average annual rate of increase of the price index was 1.5% for the entire period. The real average annual growth rate of wages and salaries was about 9.3%.

2.2 Second Period (1967-1979)

During this period, wages and salaries increased by an annual average of 14.3% in nominal terms, that is, from JD 45.4 million in 1967 to JD 303.2 million in 1979. The operating surplus increased from 63.9 million in 1967 to JD 349.1 million in 1979, an annual average rate of growth of 13.7%. Consequently, the GDP jumped from JD 131.2 million in 1967 to JD 753.0 million in 1979.

This period witnessed a sharp increase in the rate of inflation. The price index reached 299.7 points in 1973 when compared with the base year of 1967, which represented an average annual rate of increase of 9.6%. Consequently, the real annual average growth rate of wages and salaries declined from 9.3% during the first period to 4.7% during this

TABLE 2.1
Wages and Salaries, Operating Surplus and Share of Labor Return in GDP, 1952-1986

Year	Wages and Salaries [a]	Operating Surplus [a]	Domestic Factor Income	Gross Domestic Product [b]	Wage and Salaries Share in GDP (%)
1952	13.7	30.8	44.5	50.5	27.1
1953	13.7	25.1	38.8	45.5	30.2
1954	16.1	33.9	50.0	57.1	28.2
1955	17.2	27.6	44.8	52.8	32.5
1956	21.3	44.1	65.4	74.3	28.6
1957	24.0	42.3	66.3	67.1	31.5
1958	28.8	46.7	75.5	85.6	32.7
1959	23.7	32.7	65.4	93.5	24.5
1960	34.3	51.1	85.4	98.3	34.9
1961	37.6	68.9	106.5	120.1	31.3
1962	39.6	63.6	103.2	118.9	33.3
1963	42.4	69.9	112.3	129.1	32.8
1964	46.4	83.1	129.5	148.9	31.2
1965	51.8	92.5	144.3	167.6	30.9
1966	57.5	58.0	115.5	170.6	33.7
1967	45.4	53.0	109.3	131.2	34.6
1968	63.4	67.2	130.6	156.1	40.6
1969	73.2	81.6	154.8	183.4	40.0
1970	72.1	74.9	147.0	174.4	41.3
1971	74.3	83.8	158.1	186.2	40.0
1972	72.8	91.9	164.7	207.2	35.1
1973	88.6	92.0	180.6	218.3	40.5
1974	107.2	126.7	233.9	247.3	43.3
1975	120.1	140.3	260.4	312.1	38.5
1976	161.3	157.3	318.6	412.6	38.2
1977	172.2	220.1	392.3	514.2	33.5
1978	230.6	311.2	541.8	632.2	36.5
1979	303.2	349.1	652.3	753.0	40.3
1980	409.9	449.7	859.6	984.3	41.6
1981	474.1	543.3	1017.4	1164.2	40.8
1982	550.3	533.3	1078.8	1321.2	41.6
1983	604.4	528.5	1137.7	1422.7	42.5
1984	649.8	546.1	1195.9	1498.4	43.4
1985	688.9	553.9	1242.8	1605.9	42.9
1986	738.3	532.0	1269.3	1619.9	45.0

[a] In million JD, current prices.
[b] Equals the sum of wages and salaries, operating surplus, consumption of fixed capital and indirect taxes (net).

Source: Department of Statistics, National Accounts in Jordan, 1960-1986 (Amman, several years).

second period. This decline was mainly attributed to the increase in the size of the labor force as a direct result of the 1967 Arab-Israeli War, which led to an influx of 400,000 people to the East Bank of Jordan.

2.3 Third Period (1980-1986)

This period witnessed a considerable slowdown in the rate of economic growth as a result of the continued worldwide recession, which adversely affected the Middle East as a whole. During this period, wages and salaries increased from JD 409.9 million in 1980 to JD 738.3 million in 1986, and the operating surplus increased from JD 449.7 million in 1980 to JD 531.0 million in 1986. The GDP increased from JD 984.3 million in 1980 to JD 1639.9 million in 1986.

When we examine the share of labor income (wages and salaries as a proportion of GDP), we see that it increased during all three of the periods under study: from 27.1% to 33.7% for the first period; from 34.6% to 40.3% for the second period; and from 41.6% to 45.0 % for the third period (Table 2.1). Therefore, the increase in the share of labor income in the 1980s as compared with the 1970s indicated that to a certain extent there was greater equality in the distribution of personal income in the 1980s. This improvement was represented by an increase in the wage share of value added for various economic sectors (Table 2.2). Nevertheless, the rise in the overall wage share in GDP may be attributed mainly to the shift in employment from agriculture to government services.

3. Distribution of Levels of Income by Urban and by Rural Areas

The issue of distribution may not be strictly confined to income from factors of production (functional income distribution) or to personal income

TABLE 2.2
Wage Share of Value Added for Various Economic Sectors (%)

Sector	1973	1982	1986
Agriculture	10.2	14.6	26.0
Mining	50.0	32.9	31.5
Manufacturing	19.4	28.8	30.8
Construction	59.1	60.1	66.0
Transportation	42.4	43.2	46.5
Trade	17.7	23.0	26.7
Financial services	6.8	11.0	23.2
Government services	100.0	98.2	98.0

Source: Department of Statistics, *National Accounts in Jordan, 1973-1986* (Amman, several years).

(size distribution of income).

This issue also includes the distribution of wealth, particularly the distribution of ownership of the factors of production. A clear distinction between these two different concepts--wealth and income--has to be drawn. The concept of wealth refers to the cumulative factors of production accruing from the operation of capital within a specific period; the concept of income is based on measurement of the flow of income during a given period, usually one year.

No surveys on the distribution of wealth in Jordan are available except those related to the various statistical censuses undertaken by the Department of Statistics, such as the agricultural census, which shows the distribution of agricultural lands, and the housing census, which reflects the number of households. Moreover, those surveys that do pertain to income distribution are limited in scope and have not been conducted on a regular basis. Significant income distribution surveys were undertaken only in 1973, 1981, and 1982.

In general, an income distribution measure or inequality measure "is usually defined in terms of the deviation of a given distribution of income from the ideal distribution."[1] Or it is "a scalar representation of the interpersonal differences of income within a given population." [2]

Various methods and measures have been developed in an attempt to measure the relative well-being of various income recipients in any given society. These measures aim to register the overall income disparities among the total population. The prolific research aiming at summarizing inequality of income has yielded numerous measures, which can be classified in three groups: measures derived from a specific type of mathematical equation; measures of the mean deviation type, based on the statistical theory of frequency distribution; and measures constructed on theoretical criteria of welfare equivalents of individual incomes.

The Lorenz curve is among the most useful measures used to describe the concept of income distribution. It is defined as "the relationship between the cumulative proportion of income units and the cumulative proportion of income received when units are arranged in ascending order of income." [3] It follows that the slope of the Lorenz curve is always positive and increases monotonically. (See Chapter 4 for a more detailed explanation of the Lorenz inequality measure.)

The most widely used inequality measure is the Gini index. It represents the area bounded by the Lorenz curve and the line of perfect equality and is equal to the ratio of this area to the area of the triangle. The Gini coefficient falls between zero and one: Zero represents a situation of perfect equality, and one represents perfect inequality.

The few available surveys pertaining to inequality of income distribution in Jordan all demonstrate that income disparities exist among the various

TABLE 2.3
Income Distribution [a] by Urban and Rural Areas, 1973 and 1982

Area	Bottom Quintile	Second Quintile	Third Quintile	Fourth Quintile	Top Quintile
Urban					
1973	7.0	12.5	16.5	19.4	44.6
1982	6.9	10.4	17.3	24.3	41.1
Rural					
1973	7.0	12.8	18.1	23.8	38.3
1982	7.5	11.2	18.7	26.2	36.3

[a] Individual wage earners and self-employed individuals.

Sources: World Bank, *Jordan–Efficiency and Equity of Government Revenues and Social Expenditures*, 2 vols. (Washington, D.C.: July 1985, unpublished); Ghazi Assaf, *The Size Distribution of Income in Jordan in 1973* (Amman: Royal Scientific Society, June 1979); Department of Statistics, *Manpower Survey, 1982* (Amman, n.d.).

sectors of society. This fact is clearly demonstrated by the figures shown in Table 2.3, which confirms that there is inequality of income distribution in the kingdom.

Table 2.3 shows that in 1973 the income share of the top 20% of individuals in urban areas was 6.4 times greater than the share of the poorest 20%. In 1982, the income of the top 20% was 5.9 times greater than that of the lowest 20% which reflected the fact that a slight improvement in the distribution of income had occurred. As for the rural areas, a similar trend in the distribution of income for the same quintiles can be seen. Thus, the share of the top 20% in 1973 was about 5.5 times greater than that of the bottom 20%, whereas the share of the top 20% was 4.8 time greater than that of the lowest 20% in 1982.

The same analysis will be applied here to establish the comparative level of inequality of income distribution in rural areas and urban areas. When the poorest 20% in the two areas are compared, we see that in 1973 they received the same share of total income, whereas the top 20% in the urban areas acquired a share 1.2 times greater than that of the same quintile in rural areas. In contrast, by 1982 the share of the poorest 20% of the population of rural areas was about 1.1 times greater than that of the same quintile in urban areas. It should be noted here that this trend was reversed for the top 20% in the two areas. This is demonstrated by the fact that the share of the top 20% in urban areas was 1.1 times greater than the same quintile in rural areas in 1982.

The preceding analysis is confirmed when we examine the Lorenz curve, an example of which is shown in Figure 2.1. As indicated earlier, the Lorenz curve is a most useful measure for the description of inequality of income distribution. The horizontal axis reflects the cumulative number (share in percent) of households, ranked by income level, whereas the vertical axis reflects the corresponding cumulative household income.

The diagonal line represents the line of perfect equality (where 10% of the earners receive 10% of income, 80% of earners receive 80% of income, and so forth). The further the curve is skewed from the diagonal line, the greater the inequality of distribution it presents.

When we examine the Lorenz curve for 1982 (Figure 2.1), we see that in that year income distribution in the rural areas was less inequitable than in the urban areas when individual wage earners and the self-employed are taken into account. This is also confirmed by an overall low Gini coefficient of 0.2905 for rural areas as compared with 0.3286 in urban areas.

The findings of the Vocational Training Corporation Survey conducted in 1981 were broadly similar and confirmed these statistics, as shown in Table 2.4. This survey illustrated income distribution in Jordan as meas-

FIGURE 2.1
Individual and Urban Income 1982, [a] Measured
by Wages and Salaries

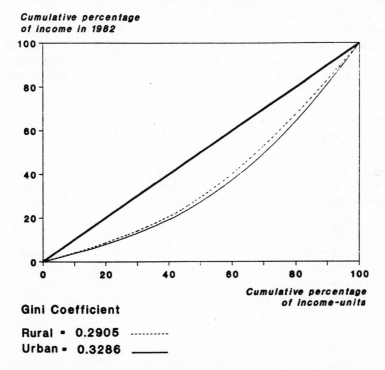

Gini Coefficient

Rural • 0.2905 ----------

Urban • 0.3286 _____

[a] Individual wage earners and self-employed persons

ured by factor income (wages and salaries, self-employed, and capital income).

Table 2.4 illustrates that in 1973 the poorest 30% of the population earned 11.5% of the total earned income in the kingdom, while the top 10% received 35.8% of total income. There had been a slight improvement for the same groups by 1981: The poorest 30% now received 11.6% as against 28.2% for the top decile.

When income distribution for 1973 is compared with that for 1981, a number of points is clear:

- The share of total income earned by the poorest 30% of population remained almost exactly the same.
- The top two deciles accounted for approximately 50% of the total income in 1973 whereas they accounted for about 44% of total income in 1981, indicating an improvement of income distribution between the years under study.
- The top decile received total income 16.3 times greater than that of the lowest 10% in 1973, whereas the situation had substantially improved by 1981, as the upper decile received income only 8.5 times greater than that of the lower decile.
- In general, there was a slight improvement in the distribution of income for all deciles in 1981 as compared with 1973, as shown by the Lorenz curve (Figure 2.2). This fact may be further illustrated by the drop in the Gini coefficient from 0.3802 in 1973 to 0.3231 in 1981.

TABLE 2.4
Income Distribution by Deciles of Income Earners, 1973 and 1981

Earners by Deciles		Percentage Share in Total Income	
		1973	1981
Bottom	10%	2.2	3.3
2nd	10%	4.1	4.1
3rd	10%	5.2	4.2
4th	10%	6.0	7.2
5th	10%	6.0	8.0
6th	10%	7.8	8.1
7th	10%	8.5	8.2
8th	10%	10.8	13.0
9th	10%	13.6	15.7
Top	10%	35.8	28.2

Sources: Ghazi Assaf, *The Size Distribution of Income in Jordan in 1973* (Amman: Royal Scientific Society, June 1979); Vocational Training Corporation, *Training and Job Opportunities for Women in Jordan* (Amman, December 1981).

FIGURE 2.2
Income Distribution by Individual, 1973 and 1981,
Measured by Factor Income

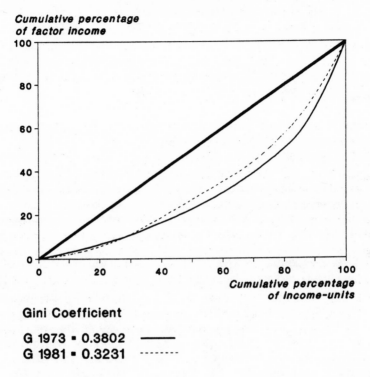

Cumulative percentage of factor income

Cumulative percentage of income-units

Gini Coefficient

G 1973 = 0.3802 ——————

G 1981 = 0.3231 ----------

4. Expenditure Distribution by Family and by Individual

Table 2.5 illustrates the inequality of expenditure distribution in Jordan for 1980. When analyzed by family, the share of the top expenditure quintile in both urban and rural areas was several times greater than that of the lowest expenditure quintiles: The top expenditure quintile in urban areas spent 6.8 times more than the lowest expenditure quintile, whereas the top expenditure quintile in the rural areas spent 7.6 times more than the lowest quintile in the same areas. This shows clearly that inequality of expenditure was higher in rural areas. This is confirmed by a higher Gini coefficient of 0.3824 in rural areas against 0.3430 for urban areas; by Table 2.6 and by Figure 2.3.

When we examine expenditure distribution by individual for the same year, we find that the lowest quintiles in both urban and rural areas had the

TABLE 2.5

Expenditure Distribution by Family and Individual, 1980

	Bottom Quintile	Second Quintile	Third Quintile	Fourth Quintile	Top Quintile
By family					
Urban	6.3	11.6	15.0	24.2	43.0
Rural	6.5	10.1	14.1	20.0	49.3
Jordan	6.0	10.0	14.6	25.1	44.2
By individual					
Urban	5.8	9.1	13.0	20.7	51.3
Rural	5.8	9.4	13.4	21.4	50.0
Jordan	5.8	9.2	13.1	20.9	51.0

Sources: Department of Statistics, *Family Expenditure Survey* (Amman, n.d.). World Bank, *Jordan--Efficiency and Equity of Government Revenues and Social Expenditures*, 2 vols. (Washington, D.C.: World Bank, July 1985, unpublished).

same level of expenditure. This also applies to the top expenditure quintile in the two areas, indicated by an almost equivalent Gini coefficient (Table 2.6) for the two areas. There was no equality of income in the two areas: The top expenditure quintiles in both rural and urban areas spent about 9 times more than the lowest expenditure quintiles in the two areas.

When we examine family expenditure distribution across the regions, we see that the share of the lowest expenditure quintile for all five governorates--Ma'an, Karak, Irbid, Balqa, and Amman--accounted for 7.6%, 6.1%, 6.6%, 6.5%, and 7.1% of total expenditure, respectively, whereas the top expenditure quintile for the same governorates accounted for 40.4%, 44.1%, 47.0%, 44.2%, and 41.7% of the total, respectively (Table 2.7).

TABLE 2.6

Expenditure Distribution by Family and Individual: Gini Coefficent, 1980

Area	Family Gini Goefficient	Individual Gini Coefficient
Urban	0.3430	0.4104
Rural	0.3824	0.4012
Jordan	0.3670	0.4080

Sources: Department of Statistics, *Family Expenditure Survey* (Amman, n.d.). World Bank, *Jordan--Efficiency and Equity of Government Revenues and Social Expenditures*, 2 vols. (Washington, D.C.: World Bank, July 1985, unpublished).

FIGURE 2.3
Rural and Urban Expenditure Distribution by Family, 1980

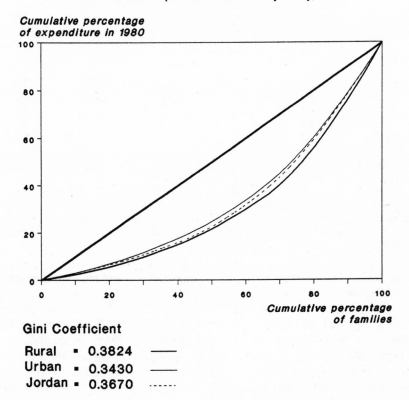

*Cumulative percentage
of expenditure in 1980*

*Cumulative percentage
of families*

Gini Coefficient

Rural ▪ 0.3824 ——
Urban ▪ 0.3430 ——
Jordan ▪ 0.3670 ------

Table 2.7 indicates that the top expenditure quintile in Ma'an spent 5.3 times more than the lowest expenditure quintile, whereas the top expenditure quintiles in Karak and Irbid spent 7.2 times more than the lower expenditure quintiles. This verifies that Ma'an governorate had the lowest level of inequality of expenditure distribution when compared with the other governorates. This is supported by the fact that this governorate also had the lowest Gini coefficient, by Table 2.8 and by Figure 2.4.

When examining regional expenditure distribution by individual, we should note that the lowest expenditure quintile for all five governorates (Ma'an, Karak, Balqa, Irbid, and Amman) accounted for 7.6%, 6.5%, 7.4%, 6.6%, and 7.3% of total expenditure, respectively. The top expenditure quintiles accounted for 42.6%, 43.4%, 43.7%, 41.6%, and 42.0% of total expenditure, respectively.

TABLE 2.7
Expenditure Distribution by Governorate, 1980

	Bottom Quintile	Second Quintile	Third Quintile	Fourth Quintile	Top Quintile
By family					
Ma'an	7.6	11.8	16.5	23.6	40.4
Karak	6.1	11.5	15.9	22.3	44.1
Balqa	6.5	10.4	15.1	23.7	44.2
Irbid	6.6	10.5	14.8	21.0	47.0
Amman	7.1	10.9	15.5	24.8	41.7
By individual					
Ma'an	7.6	11.3	15.9	22.6	42.6
Karak	6.5	11.4	16.0	22.7	43.4
Balqa	7.4	11.1	15.7	25.1	40.7
Irbid	6.6	11.0	15.7	25.1	41.6
Amman	7.3	10.8	15.4	24.5	42.0

Sources: Department of Statistics, *Family Expenditure Survey ,1980* (Amman, n.d.). World Bank, *Jordan–Efficiency and Equity of Government Revenues and Social Expenditures*, 2 vols. (Washington, D.C.: World Bank, July 1985, unpublished).

This demonstrates that the top expenditure quintiles in Ma'an and Balqa spent 5.6 and 5.5 times more than the lowest expenditure quintiles, respectively, whereas the top expenditure quintiles in both Karak and Irbid spent 6.7 and 6.3 times more than the lowest expenditure quintiles, respectively. This indicates that inequality of expenditure was more pronounced in Karak and Irbid than in Ma'an and Balqa, which is supported by the higher Gini coefficients for Karak and Irbid.

TABLE 2.8
Gini Coefficient by Governorate, 1980

Governorate	Family Gini Coefficient	Individual Gini Coefficient
Ma'an	0.3097	0.3250
Karak	0.3476	0.3404
Balqa	0.3548	0.3233
Irbid	0.3654	0.3361
Amman	0.3321	0.3325

Sources: Department of Statistics, *Family Expenditures Survey , 1980* (Amman, n.d.). World Bank, *Jordan–Efficiency and Equity of Government Revenues and Social Expenditures,* 2 vols.   (Washington, D.C.: World Bank, July 1985, unpublished).

FIGURE 2.4
Expenditure Distribution per Family by Governorate, 1980

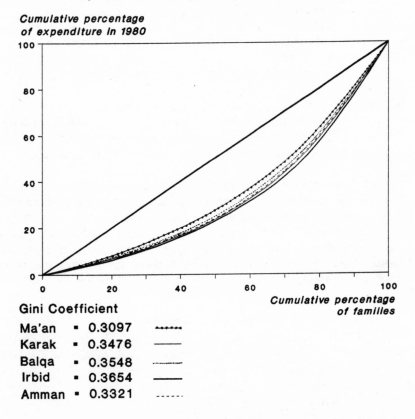

*Cumulative percentage
of expenditure in 1980*

*Cumulative percentage
of families*

Gini Coefficient

Ma'an	▪	0.3097	····
Karak	▪	0.3476	———
Balqa	▪	0.3548	————
Irbid	▪	0.3654	———
Amman	▪	0.3321	- - - - -

5. Factors Contributing to Inequality
of Income Distribution

Numerous factors have contributed to the existing inequality of income distribution in Jordan. Following is a brief exposition of these factors:

- The pursuit of certain financial policies has tended, to favor entrepreneurs, landowners, and real estate owners at the expense of employees and tenants. For instance, tax exemptions and subsidies extended to capital investments have played a major role in enhancing the share of entrepreneurs in the national income.
- Land distribution policies have contributed significantly to inequality of income among the various sectors of the population. Such policies have led to the concentration of land among a smaller proportion of the population.

- The system of taxation has also contributed to a certain extent to the inequality of income distribution. Indirect taxes are imposed on all Jordanian nationals on an equal basis, irrespective of their varying incomes. But tax evasion is more common among higher income groups, while the upper middle income groups bear the highest relative burden of direct taxation. The income tax base remains seriously eroded as a result of both legal tax exemption and tax evasion.
  - Limitation of import licences and franchise licences to a restricted group of people has provided increasing opportunities for the rich to add to its wealth, while the relative income of poor people has deteriorated as the gap between the two sectors has widened.

Other important factors include rural-urban migration, a tendency among Jordanians to choose academic education at the expense of vocational education, certain social habits such as marriage and fertility, the concentration of public services in the major cities that has resulted from biased development efforts in favor of urban areas, and the influx of large numbers of people from the occupied West Bank to the East Bank of Jordan as a result of the Arab-Israeli conflict.

6. Poverty in Jordan

Poverty can in general be defined "as a situation in which needs are not sufficiently satisfied."[4] In any country, poverty is regarded as a relative phenomenon reflecting the economic condition of the unfortunate groups as compared with other, more fortunate groups in society. Absolute poverty refers to an individual's inability to attain the absolute basic needs of life, whereas relative poverty refers to the share of low income groups in overall income.

The standard method of measuring poverty is to define a poverty line below which people are considered poor. The poverty line is normally defined as the income level that enables people to secure a minimum standard of living: the subsistence level. Recently, however, poverty lines have been drawn according to rather more objective criteria, such as nutritional needs for human survival defined as minimum necessary daily caloric or protein intake; the minimum income below which a person cannot buy the basic requirements of food, shelter, and clothing; the minimum wage rate; and the level of income below which an average person cannot save.

In defining the poverty line in any given country, numerous difficulties may arise with reference to cultural, regional, and consumer tastes, which vary from one region to another. Difficulties may also arise because of the variation in prices and costs of goods and services across the different regions of the world.

6.1 Poverty Measurement in Jordan

In specifying the poverty line in Jordan, one useful approach is to measure the cost of minimum nutritional requirements. To allow for minimum shelter, an amount equivalent to 20-30% of this measure is added. The sum of the two components constitutes the poverty line measure.

Because no detailed information on minimum nutritional requirements in Jordan is available, my estimate will rely on data derived from the international standard that specifies minimum nutritional needs of 2304-2497 calories on a daily basis. [5] These minimum calories have been estimated to cost JD 10.8 each month. The addition of 30% to this sum brings the individual minimum monthly income to JD 14.04. Consequently, the poverty line in Jordan is estimated to be about JD 94.1 per family per month, when the average family size of 6.7 persons is taken into account $(14.04 \times 6.7 = 94.1)$.

Similar findings were reached by the Arab Industrial Development Center, which estimates the minimum dietary and shelter requirements to cost JD 17.3. This estimate means that the relative poverty line is approximately JD 115.5 per family per month: $17.3 \times 6.7 = 115.9$. This calculation indicates that the poverty line in Jordan is situated in the range of JD 94 to JD 116 per family per month. The number of people whose incomes fall below the relative poverty line is estimated at between 20% and 25% of the total population. It follows that the number of families living in absolute poverty is between 87,000 and 108,000 families $(2.9 \times 0.2 \times 1/6.7 = 87; 2.9 \times 0.25 \times 1/6.7 = 108)$.

6.2 Policies and Measures for Poverty Eradication

With the exception of the National Assistance Fund, adequate measures and programs addressing the eradication of poverty have not been established by the concerned authorities. Measures already taken have included the importing and pricing of basic commodities; the provision of direct subsidies for certain commodities (wheat, flour, rice, and sugar), and the establishment of civil and military consumer service corporations.

The Ministry of Social Development provides cash subsidies to certain categories of the poor: the aged, orphans and foster children, mentally and physically handicapped individuals, and emergency cases. The amount of this subsidy ranges from JD 4 to JD 12 per month for each family.

The Five-Year Plan for Social and Economic Development (1986-1990) demonstrated that there was an increasing realization of the vital importance of eliminating poverty in Jordan. To this end, the plan called for the establishment of a national assistance fund project to draw up a plan that would be implemented in stages depending on government capabilities and the means of voluntary and private agencies. The primary aim of the plan would be to arrest the growth of poverty; the secondary aim would be to help needy families set up small, productive enterprises on an individual or group basis. In cases of disability or other constraints, the fund provided monthly financial assistance. The cost of this fund was estimated at JD 19.5 million to be disbursed during the period 1986-1990.

7. Summary and Recommendations

This chapter explored in analytical terms the nature and magnitude of problems of income distribution and poverty in Jordan. The analysis indicated that income disparities exist among the various sectors of the population, particularly between urban and rural areas in the kingdom. The disparities between the upper and lower deciles are even greater than the interregional disparities and are a clear indication of inequality in income distribution. Although inhibited by the lack of available data, the chapter nevertheless indicated that many Jordanians still live in absolute poverty, which reflects the fact that the benefits of economic growth have not reached all groups of society and all regions of the country in an equitable manner. To deal with such crucial issues, the following recommendations are put forward:

- Issues of income distribution and poverty in Jordan have not received the attention they deserve. A comprehensive empirical survey should be carried out to establish where the poor are to be found, the nature of poverty, and its causes. Regularly updated surveys are urgently needed.
- The distribution of the benefits of development among the various sectors of the population in both rural and urban areas should be reviewed with the objective of balancing out the gains of development throughout the kingdom.
- A broad strategy in the spirit of "poverty elimination" should be adopted. This could be approached initially through increasing efforts to integrate or merge organizations tailored for poverty eradication.
- Financial assistance extended by the Ministry of Social Development and other related organizations should be expanded, both by increasing the number of recipients and by increasing the amount of financial assistance given to them. As currently constituted, such assistance is negligible and limited in its effects; the cash value of such financial

assistance has remained unchanged during the last few years.
- Employment opportunities that lead to an increase in the participation of women in the Jordanian labor force should be developed in order to reduce the dependency ratio and increase the average monthly income per household (in 1985, women accounted for only 12.5% of the total labor force). This, in its turn, would reduce the number of poor families.
- The reduction or elimination of poverty requires a reduction in the inequality of income distribution by raising the income of the lowest income groups relative to those of the highest income groups. This means that poverty can be eliminated if general economic progress raises the share of productive assets owned by the lower income groups while reducing the share of the higher income groups.
- The human capital of the poor must be protected by guaranteeing the poor's access to health and education services. Therefore, medical care facilities and educational establishments should be improved.

Notes

1. Kakwani, N.C.: *Income Inequality and Poverty* (Oxford: 1980), p. 53.
2. Cowell, A.F.: *Measuring Inequality* (Oxford: 1977), p. 9.
3. Ibid., p. 30.
4. Hagenaars, A.J.M.: *The Perception of Poverty* (New York: Oxford University Press, 1986), p. 1.
5. *Al-Dustour*, February 1, 1986, p. 10.

Bibliography

Abu Sheikha, A: "Income Distribution and Poverty in Jordan." In Abu Jaber, Kamel (ed.): *Major Issues in Jordanian Development.* Amman: Queen Alia Social Welfare Fund, 1983.

Adelman, I., and Robinson, S.: *Income Distribution Policy in Developing Countries: A Case Study of Korea.* Oxford: Oxford University Press, 1978.

Assaf, G.: *The Size Distribution of Income in Jordan in 1973.* Amman: Royal Scientific Society, June 1979.

Cowell, A.F.: *Measuring Inequaltiy.* Oxford: Oxford University Press, 1977.

Dajani, J.S.: "Poverty and Income Distribution in Jordan." *Banks of Jordan Magazine* 1 (1982).

Department of Statistics: *Family Expenditure Survey, 1980.* Amman, n.d..

_____ : *Manpower Survey, 1982.* Amman, n.d..

_____ : *National Accounts in Jordan, 1959-1966, 1967-1977, 1978-1982, 1981-1986.* Amman, several years.

Fellner, W., and Haley, B.F.: *Reading in the Theory of Income Distribution.* London: Allen and Unwin, 1961.

Hagenaars, A.J.M.: *The Perception of Poverty.* New York: Oxford University Press,

1986.

Jordan Development Board: *Seven Year Program for Economic Development, 1964-1970.* Amman, 1965.

Kakwani, N.C.: *Income Inequality and Poverty: Methods of Estimation and Policy Applications.* Oxford: Oxford University Press, 1980.

Ministry of Planning: *Five Year Plan for Economic and Social Development, 1981-1985.* Amman, 1981.

_____: *Five Year Plan for Economic and Social Development, 1986-1990.* Amman, 1986.

National Planning Council: *Three Year Development Plan, 1973-1975.* Amman, 1972.

Shaban, Radwan Ali: "Expenditure Distribution and Poverty in Jordan." Philadelphia: University of Pennsylvania, June 1987, unpublished.

Tarawneh, Fayez: "Poverty and the Distribution of Growth in Jordan." *Banks of Jordan Magazine* 3, Amman (1983).

Vocational Training Corporation: *Training and Job Opportunities for Women in Jordan.* Amman, December 1981.

World Bank: *Jordan--Efficiency and Equity of Government Revenues and Social Expenditure.* 2 Vols. Washington, D.C.: World Bank, Report no. 5697-Jo., July 1985, unpublished.

3

Determinants of Inequality
in Economic Development

Fayez A.Tarawneh

1. Introduction

Jordan has one of the very few economies that was able to achieve double-digit growth rates in the second half of the 1970s. Its gross domestic product grew by more than 12% during the period 1975-1980. This growth in output was not an isolated phenomenon; development was extended to all aspects of social and economic life. Infrastructural services such as piped water, electricity, and roads were extensively improved such that they reached more than 90% of the population. Social services witnessed a similar improvement as school enrollment in the compulsory cycle became universal and as health services reached the remotest of the rural population centers.

Given this remarkable social and economic development, little concern was given to wealth distribution. The same held true for the size distribution of income. As every member of society became better off, measurement of the discrepancies in the level at which they enjoyed the benefits of development was not felt to be pressing. Consequently, very few studies were carried out on changes in the distribution of income during the 1970s and 1980s and even those gave conflicting results.

Since the early 1980s, the Jordanian economy has witnessed a marked slowing in its economic growth rates. As a result, various sectors of the population have come to the attention of planners and policymakers. Distributional issues of development have once again been at the forefront of economic concerns. A regional planning program was launched in 1986 to partially deal with such issues.

This chapter will attempt to contribute to distributional issues in Jordan through the elaboration of a theoretical framework that will help the reader understand the interlinked and complex relationships that affect the distribution of income in general. By now it is well known that the classical doctrine, which stated that the primary solution to poverty and inequality of distribution was economic development, has been challenged by recent empirical evidence suggesting that inequality of income is increasing rather than decreasing, even in countries with rapid development.

Although the distribution of income has become an integral part of economic theory, the economist can hardly play the role of sociologist and political scientist. Yet in addressing the issue of income distribution as an economic problem, the economist cannot ignore the role of noneconomic variables and must search for some tentative propositions that can be further tested by economists and noneconomists alike. This choice is dictated as much by the magnitude and importance of the problems as by the availability of relevant information.

This chapter will attempt to identify the economic and social variables that affect income distribution as a country undergoes the process of development. Such a process leads to various structural changes that have different effects on the distribution of income and the changes therein as time passes. Logically, these structural changes are not necessarily confined to economic factors but include various noneconomic factors as well.

These variables are income, demography, employment structure, human capital, and structure of production. The direct and indirect channels through which these variables can affect the distribution of income will be explained. But income distribution in turn affects these variables either directly or through association with other variables. Hence, based on the a priori expectations of such relations, this chapter intends to draw some tentative conclusions about the valency of the direct and indirect relationships among the different variables of the model. A simultaneous equation model will be formulated in which income inequality and the foregoing structural variables will be determined simultaneously. The empirical testing of such a model will be left to future research.

2. Economic Development and Income Inequality

The relationship between income inequality and economic development can be analyzed on many levels, such as the nonlinear secular effect of income per capita on the distribution of income, the short-term relationship between income inequality and the rate of growth of such income, and the long-term relationship between income inequality and economic development. Economists have customarily utilized all the explanatory variables for income inequality in a single multiple regression equation. The choice of these independent variables is usually based on two factors: the availability of the data and some a priori expectations as to how these variables may affect income inequality. But such specifications do not guarantee the reliability of the specified hypothesis inasmuch as the regression equation may be subject to different kinds of statistical problems. Important among such problems are multicollinearity and simultaneous equations bias. In addition, the ordinary least-square (OLS) technique only demonstrates the effect of the independent variables on the dependent variable; the technique neglects causation in the other direction as well as the indirect relation through association with other variables.

In an attempt to overcome such biases and increase understanding of the determinants of the distribution of income, I will extend the traditional multiple regression single equation approach to a system of simultaneous equations in which income inequality together with some other structural variables will be determined simultaneously.

3. The Model

The major problem in any study of the determinants of the distribution of income is the formulation of a model that explicitly specifies those independent variables that must be considered determinants of income inequality. Obviously, such a specification is governed by the existence of an underlying theory that indicates that the relationship between each independent variable and the dependent variable exists and is of a particular form.

3.1 Variables

The purpose of the model is to investigate the effect of certain variables that reflect structural changes on income inequality within a simultaneous equation system. The variables are classified as follows:

- Income
  G: Income inequality (inequality coefficient)
  PCY: Real per capita income
  RCY: Rate of growth of real per capita income
- Demography
  RGP: Rate of population growth
  F: Fertility rate
  M: Mortality rate
  NM: Net migration
- Employment Structure
  FL: Female labour force participation rate
- Human Capital
  L: Literacy rate
- Structure of Production

SYA: Share of agricultural income in total income
URB: Urbanization rate
FC: Percentage of cultivated land fertilized

3.2   The Basic Equation: The Change in
Income Inequality

The basic equation of the model is that of income inequality (represented by income inequality coefficient--the Gini coefficient for simplicity). I hypothesize the following function for changes in G.

$$dG = f(dPCY, dSYA, dFL, dL, RGP) \qquad (1)$$

Income inequality is made a function of real per capita income; the share of agricultural output in total output--representing the productive structure; the female labor force participation rate--representing the employment structure; basic education or the literacy rate--representing changes in the quality of human capital; and population growth--representing demographic pressures. The value dG of the dependent variable, income inequality change, is made a function of a change of the independent variables mentioned, this change being symbolized by small letter "d". It is not the absolute values of PCY, SYA, FL or L but their increase or decrease that determines the change of inequality.

• Hypothesis 1a: A negative relation between dPCY and dG.

Cross-sectional empirical studies have shown a higher G in relatively low income countries, and longitudinal studies have confirmed the inverted U shape relationship between G and PCY for a large group of less-developed countries (LDCs).

• Hyp 1b: A negative relation between dSYA and dG.

The effect of SYA on G can be explained using the decomposition technique. The change in G can be broken down into changes in G within individual sectors, the change in the income share of sectors, and changes in G across sectors. The effect of the change in income share of any particular sector is captured in the second and third effects.
Let us consider first the share effect. The change in the income share of any sector means a change in its relative importance and, therefore, a change in its contribution to total income inequality. If the relative importance of a particular sector increases, then its contribution to total inequality will also increase. Because income inequality in the agricultural sector is expected to be higher than inequalities in other sectors, there

is a positive relation between SYA and G. Nevertheless, SYA has a negative effect on income inequality. When the between-sector changes in G are considered, as SYA increases, the gap between the agricultural and nonagricultural sectors narrows and G tends to decrease.

In the case of Jordan, the SYA is relatively low, and inequality between the agricultural sector and the nonagricultural sectors is relatively high. Thus, I expect the second negative relation to dominate the first positive relation between SYA and G.

- Hyp 1c: A negative relation between dFL and dG.

Any increase in FL will increase family income and reduce the dependency of female family members on the income of males.

- Hyp 1d: A negative relation between dL and dG.

The basic premise of the human capital theory is that variations in labor income are due, in part, to differences in labor quality in terms of the amount of human capital acquired by the workers. Accordingly, improvements in basic education have been considered a major method for reducing income inequality, even if investment in other more specialized or higher education might raise inequality by increasing inequality in the distribution of the capital stock. Adelman and Morris (1973), Ahluwalia (1976), and Van Ginneken (1975) all found a statistically significant negative relationship between literacy and income inequality for a wide range of LDCs.

- Hyp 1e: An ambiguous relation between RGP and dG.

Population growth affects the aggregate labor supply directly; in particular, it affects the allocation of individuals to different income categories. With high rates of population growth, income inequality may tend to rise because a larger portion of the labor force will be trapped in low income employment, especially in the traditional sectors of the economy (Ahluwalia, 1976). We can argue, however, that a higher population growth rate means a higher demand for food, which in turn leads to improvements across the board in favor of the agricultural sector. Such improvements should narrow the gap between the agricultural and the nonagricultural sectors and result in lower overall income inequality. Nevertheless, such incentives could have an adverse effect on inequality within the agricultural sector because large commercial farmers would benefit more than the others.

Hence, the predicted sign of the relationship between RGP and G is ambiguous. In fact, it is problematical to predict the impact of population growth on the distribution of income because, in addition to the possible effects mentioned previously, the rate of population growth is the net effect of fertility rates, mortality rates, and migration (in and out) where each of these variables has an indirect impact on income inequality through association with other determinants of income distribution. This point will be explained more fully.

The specification of equation (1) raises two important questions. First, what are the indirect effects on G of those variables included in equation (1) (through association with other variables not included in that equation)? Second, does G exert any kind of influence on such variables? To answer these questions, the simultaneous equation model will consider all variables included in equation (1), together with some other variables, as endogenous.

3.3   Other Behavioral Equations

3.3.1 Changes in Real Per Capita Income

$$dPCY = f(dURB, dFL, dL) \tag{2}$$

• Hyp 2a: An ambiguous relation between dURB and dPCY.

The change in the rate of urbanization represents the displacement of the rural labor force to the urban sector. Because fertility rates are usually higher in rural areas than in urban areas, the displaced labor may be considered part of what is called "surplus labor": those workers who can be considered economically unexploited resources of the rural sector. In the context of the surplus labor theory (Lewis, 1954), this displacement will not cause any loss of agricultural output because surplus workers are assumed to have marginal or zero productivity. At the same time, industrial output will increase because the need for additional labor in that sector will be satisfied.

But if those workers who migrate from the rural to the urban areas are not marginal workers, then the net effect of urbanization on total output is the net effect of the loss in agricultural output combined with the gains in nonagricultural output, assuming that the migrants eventually join the labor force in urban areas.

• Hyp 2b: A positive relation between dFL and dPCY.

The traditional activities of females, especially the services of housewives, are usually omitted from national income accounts because these activities are nonmarketable and difficult to measure. Hence, when the participation of females in the labor market increases, total measured income will also increase.

- Hyp 2c: A positive relation between dL and dPCY.

According to the human capital approach, basic education or literacy will not only reduce income inequality but will also raise income. All three variables (dURB, dFL, dL) included in equation (2) are endogenous variables expressed in the following functions.

3.3.2 Changes in Urbanization Rate

$$dURB = f(dPCY, dSYA, dNM) \qquad (3)$$

- Hyp 3a: A positive relation between dPCY and dURB.

As economic development proceeds and per capita income increases, the rate of the urbanization will increase because of the continual movement of rural workers to the urban sector.

- Hyp 3b: A negative relation between dSYA and dURB.

The higher the income share of the agricultural sector is, the lower the urbanization rate will be because of lower economic incentives for rural-urban migration.

- Hyp 3c: A positive relation between dNM and dURB.

Net migration is expected to be positively related to urbanization because the migrants usually settle in the urban areas.

3.3.3 Changes in Female Labor Force
Participation Rate

$$dFL = f(dPCY, dURB, dL, dF) \qquad (4)$$

- Hyp 4a: A positive relation between dPCY and dFL.

It may seem logical to argue that FL should drop as economic development proceeds and income increases because women's need to join the labor force and supplement family income will decrease; yet with the better employment opportunities for women that arise with development, rates of pay for females are to be expected to increase, thereby inducing more females to join the labor force.

• Hyp 4b: A positive relation between dURB and dFL.

The need for females to work may be higher in urban areas because of higher living costs; higher returns on saving and investment than in the rural areas will act as a further inducement. Also, the social and traditional barriers for females who engage in market activities are usually less restrictive, and the range of opportunities for employment is relatively more attractive in urban areas than in rural areas.

• Hyp 4c: A positive relation between dL and dFL.

According to Standing (1978), education, especially that of females, allows females to enter the labor market more freely because they can compete more successfully with men in certain jobs. Education may also change the attitudes of females toward participation in the labor force. Additionally when females are educated, the opportunity cost of their not working will increase accordingly, thereby inducing such females to join the labor force.

• Hyp 4d: A negative relation between dF and dFL.

Probably the most important variable effecting FL is the fertility rate. Obviously, F affects the level of participation of married women in the fertile age group in the labor force, and, in particular, the participation of those who are educated because the opportunity cost is higher for them than for the uneducated (Enke, 1963, 1971; Weintraub, 1962). The predicted sign is negative because in all societies without exception the role of child bearing and rearing devolves to women and makes highly intensive demands on their time. In LDCs, however, there may be relatively close substitutes for the mother as caretaker-- for example, older siblings and other relatives living within the extended family or low cost servants. Hence, the effect of child bearing and rearing may be relatively weak in the LDC context.

3.3.4 The Change in the Literacy Rate

$$dL = f(dPCY, dURB, dNM) \tag{5}$$

• Hyp 5a: A positive relation between dPCY and dL.

As per capita income increases, both the supply of and the demand for education tend to increase. On the supply side, the number and quality of public and private schools increase as the level of income increases, and on the demand side, people can afford this kind of investment in human capital and can delay current employment as income increases.

- Hyp 5b: A positive relation between dURB and dL.

With a higher rate of urbanization, the need for more schooling and for a more educated labor force and personnel increases to meet the more highly technical and specialized jobs in urban areas.

- Hyp 5c: An ambiguous relation between dNM and dL.

The effect of net migration on literacy depends on the relative level of education of the migrants.

3.3.5 Changes in Share of Agricultural Income

$$dSYA = f(dPCY, dURB, dFC) \tag{6}$$

- Hyp 6a: An ambiguous relation between dPCY and dSYA.

As income increases, the demand for food will increase, which will in turn increase agricultural income. We can argue, however, that because the demand for agricultural products is income inelastic, an increase in income will not initiate any changes in agricultural income or may in fact reduce it.

- Hyp 6b: A negative relation between dURB and dSYA.

The effect of URB on SYA is expected to have a negative sign, especially if it is assumed that those who migrate to the urban areas are the nonmarginal agricultural workers.

- Hyp 6c: A straightforward, positive relation between dFC and dSYA.

3.3.6 Population Growth

$$RGP = f (F_t, F_{t-1}, M_t, M_{t-1}, dNM) \tag{7}$$

Both F_{t-1} and M_{t-1} are considered exogenous variables, while F_t, M_t, and NM are endogenous variables specified as follows.

3.3.7 Fertility Rate

$$F_t = f\ (PCY_t,\ G_t,\ FL_t,\ L_t,\ M_t,\ M_{t-1},\ URB_t,\ F_{t-1}) \tag{8}$$

- Hyp 8a: A negative relation between PCY_t and F_t.

In the theory of fertility, the behavior of families in determining the number of births they desire is considered rational in the sense that they tend to balance the utilities derived from all additional birth against the costs of having this birth (Gregory, Compbell, and Cheny, 1972; Leibenstein, 1957; Shultz, 1973). As income increases, the need for children as productive agents and as potential sources of security declines and as a result so, too, does the utility derived from them in these capacities. But the ability to support children and hence to obtain the extra utility they provide also increases. Moreover, because there may be preferences for children of a certain sex, and as the complementary goods necessary for a child's development (and hence the satisfaction derived from observing such development) are more readily available with higher income, it is possible that the relationship could be positive.

The cost of having an additional child is positively related to the level of income. First, the direct cost of maintaining a child is a function of the level of income of the family and its status in the social hierarchy, and therefore, it is to be expected that such cost will increase as income increases. Hence, fertility varies inversely with income as quality expenditure per child increases to the extent that parents will tend to reduce their demand for children. Second, as economic development trickles down, more market opportunities are open for women, and furthermore, a higher degree of economic mobility toward urban areas is needed for both sexes. This new occupational environment limits the number of children to minimize the cost of the parents sacrificing these new economic opportunities (or, by the same token, to maximize the social and economic mobility of the family unit).

- Hyp 8b: A positive relation between G_t and F_t.

The opportunity cost of having an additional child is higher for high income groups than for low income groups. Therefore, the more unequal the distribution of income is, the higher the fertility rate is.

- Hyp 8c: A negative relation between FL_t and F_t.

- Hyp 8d: A negtive relation between URB_t and F_t.

As explained earlier, the new occupational environment created by economic development (market opportunities for women and economic movement toward urban areas) tends to limit the number of children.

- Hyp 8e: A negative relation between L_t and F_t.

The negative direct effect is explained by two facts. First, educated couples are usually concerned with the quality rather than the quantity of their children. Second, educated couples are able to achieve greater contraceptive efficiency. The negative indirect effect is explained through association with income and female labor force participation rate. As education increases, income tends to increase, which in turn increases the direct cost of raising children. In addition, the opportunity cost of having a child increases because the wife's time becomes more valuable as her level of education increases--that is, education makes participation in the labor force more attractive.

- Hyp 8f: A positive relation between M_t and F_t.

The infant mortality rate is expected to play an important role in the decision of parents to maintain a certain family size. The higher the mortality rate is, the higher the fertility rate is. Because fertility rates usually lag behind mortality rates (Leibenstein, 1957), M_{t-1} is also included to reflect the fact that the impact of any improvement on the chances of survival is not likely to be felt immediately. It follows that past mortality rates may affect current fertility rates.

- Hyp 8g: A positvie relation between F_{t-1} and F_t.

This relation is reflection of the tendency to maintain a consistent social attitude toward fertility.

3.3.8 Mortality Rate

$$M_t = f (PCY_t, G_t, L_t) \tag{9}$$

- Hyp 9a: A negative relation between PCY_t and M_t.

- Hyp 9b: A positive relation between G_t and M_t.

As the level of income rises and its distribution becomes more equal, health care will probably become more widespread and reach more areas. In addition, the quality of health services may also improve.

● Hyp 9c: A negative relation between L_t and M_t.

When they have a higher level of education, people are more willing to accept modern methods of medical care and are more open to information about diet, personal hygiene, and the effects of such factors on their own health as well as on that of their children.

3.3.9 Changes in Net Migration

$$dNM = f(dPCY, dG, dL, dURB, RGP_{t-1}) \tag{10}$$

● Hyp 10a: A positive relation between dPCY and dNM.

● Hyp 10b: A positive relation between dG and dNM.

● Hyp 10c: A positive relation between dL and dNM.

● Hyp 10d: A positive relation between dURB and dNM.

● Hyp 10e: A positive relation between RGP_{t-1} and dNM.

It is to be expected that people will tend to move to higher income regions where income inequality is only moderate. Also, regions with higher standards of education and higher rates of urbanization are expected to receive greater inflows of people. A positive relation between lagged population growth and net migration is also expected.

3.4 Identities

To complete the model the following identities are included:

$$G_t = G_{t-1} + dG \tag{11}$$

$$L_t = L_{t-1} + dL \tag{12}$$

$$PCY_t = PCY_{t-1} + dPCY \tag{13}$$

$$FL_t = FL_{t-1} + dLF \tag{14}$$

$$URB_t = URB_{t-1} + dURB \tag{15}$$

$$dF = F_t - F_{t-1} \tag{16}$$

4. The Simultaneous Equation System

4.1 Variables

The simultaneous equation system specified previously consists of sixteen endogenous variables in sixteen equations (ten structural equations and six identities) and nine exogenous variables. Thus, the model is comprehensive. The variables of the model are:

Endogenous variables: dG, G_t, $dPCY$, PCY_t, $dSYA$, dFL, FL_t, dL, L_t, $dURB$, URB_t, RGP, M_t, dF, F_t, dNM.

Exogenous variables: G_{t-1}, PCY_{t-1}, FL_{t-1}, L_{t-1}, URB_{t-1}, RGP_{t-1}, F_{t-1}, M_{t-1}, dFC.

All equations of the model are overidentified because the number of exogenous variables excluded from each equation is greater than the number of endogenous variables included less one. The structured variables are in the form of their change over time to reflect the dynamic, or at least the comparatively static, nature of the analysis.

4.2 Indirect Relations

The focus of the model is the effect of structural variables, representing economic development, on the distribution of income. Five of these effects on G have been specified in equation (1), where the effects of PCY, SYA, FL, L, and RPG and the directions of these effects have been hypothesized by hypotheses 1a, 1b, 1c, 1d, and 1e.

We can draw tentative conclusions about the indirect relationship between the remaining four structural variables-- urbanization rate (URB), fertility rate (F), mortality rate (M), and net migration (NM)--and the distribution of income (G).

4.2.1 Effect of URB on G

According to the model's hypothesis, the following relations between a change in urbanization and changes in the variables PCY, SYA, FL, and L hold, which in turn affect income inequality G.

a. URB up changes PCY upward *or* downward, which in turn influences G in opposite direction (hypotheses 3a, 1a).
b. URB up leads to SYA down, and SYA down leads to G up (hypotheses 6b, 1b).
c. URB up leads to FL up, which in turn leads to G down (hypotheses 4b, 1c).
d. URB up leads to L up, and L up leads to G down (hyptheses 5d, 1d).

Thus, an increase in urbanization affects income inequality ambiguously, unless the forces in (a), (c), and (d) that lead to decrease in G outweigh the opposite forces in (a) and (b).

4.2.2 Effect of F on G

The direction of this indirect effect on income inequality is ambiguous as well, as can be seen from the following sequences:

a. F up forces FL down, which in turn brings G up (hypotheses 8b, 1c).
b. F up straightforward leads to RGP up, but this has an ambiguous effect on G (hypothesis 1c).

Unless the positive forces in (a) and (b) combine to outweigh the negative in (b), an increase in fertility rate does not necessarily increase income inequality.

4.2.3 Effect of M on G

The indirect effect of an increase in the mortality rate takes place via RGP and F. It is ambiguous because both an increase in RGP and in F have an ambiguous effect on G.

4.2.4 Effect of NM on G

Finally, the indirect effect of an increase in net migration is ambiguous. This result is derived from the sequences:

a. NM up leads to URB up (hypothesis 3c), having an ambiguous effect on G according to the respective sequences mentioned previously.
b. NM up changes L upward *or* downward, and L up changes G upward *or* downward (hypotheses 5c, 1d).

To sum up, the model leads to qualifications about the indirect relationship between URB, F, M, NM, and income inequality that are basically inconclusive. Empirical input will make the difference.

4.3 Model Results and Empirical Testing

The empirical testing of the specified model is left for further research, which should provide a firm base for policy recommendations. But based on a priori expectations and personal observation, we can conclude that the process of economic development leads to various kinds of structural change that exert different effects on the distribution of income and the changes therein over time. Such structural change factors are not necessarily confined to economic factors but include various noneconomic factors as well. The variables that represent improvements in the structures of production and employment and in human capital seem to play a significant double role; they contribute toward larger increases in income per capital and help to slow down the increasing trend in income inequality. Demographic pressures, however, tend to accelerate the trend toward inequality.

If productivity is associated with education, then the surplus labor theory must be rejected if it is literate citizens who move from one region to another or to urban areas within regions. If changes in urbanization contribute to increases in per capita income, then the variation in the trends of income inequality between the different regions can cause the movement toward higher stages of economic development to accelerate but at the expense of the agricultural sector, whose share in total income is reduced as the urbanization rate increases.

5. Outlook on Jordan

The process of social and economic development in Jordan was remarkable in all its aspects, and it resulted in numerous structural changes that in effect gave Jordan a new face and look. Thus, Jordan stands to be an interesting case for in-depth study and analysis of the distributional effects of growth and development. In such a study, we would expect interesting results and even at some points a departure from empirical evidence because the *structural changes* associated with development were both dynamic and comprehensive, thus covering a wide range of sectoral and regional areas.

Although income distribution has always occupied a sizable portion of the economic, social, and political thinking of Jordanian decisionmakers, this important variable has always stood at a distance from deep analysis and has never been supported by comprehensive empirical research. In sum, little has been done to incorporate the distribution of income as an *endogenous variable* in the Jordanian planning models.

The application of the simultaneous equation model developed in this chapter could serve as a base for analyzing and further extending the understanding of the determinants of the distribtuion of income. Such an application could also explain the causal relationship between income inequality and the selected socioeconomic variables representing the structural changes associated with development.

Whether the inverted U shape relationship between *income inequality* and *income per capita* is confirmed or rejected is an empirical question. We would expect, however, that the inverted U hypothesis is confirmed for the case of Jordan due to the speedy pace of social and economic development and, more importantly, due to direct positive effects of the regional development efforts exerted in the implementation of the three five-year plans since 1975.

The direct and indirect effects of the other structural variables on the distribtuion of income are less obvious. The high rate of *population growth* in Jordan--due to a high fertility rate, a low mortality rate, and high rates of immigration--is associated with a high degree of concentration of population in the *urban areas*, particularly in the Greater Amman district. It is mainly the *literate worker* who migrates from the rural areas to the cities, leaving the agricultural sector heavily dependent on foreign labor and at the same time increasing the level of unemployment in the urban areas. Such pressures exert negative effects on the distribution of income.

Nevertheless, the low cost of foreign labor in the agricultural sector, together with the specialized regional agricultural projects in the Jordan Valley and other areas in the kingdom, has helped in maintaining, or slightly increasing, the relative *share of the agricultural income* in total income. Thus, I expect a positive impact of the variables representing the structure of production on income distribution. Both the high literacy rate, representing the human capital, and the increasing *female labor force* participation rate, representing the employment structure, have positive influence on the distribution of income, directly reducing overall income inequality.

References

Adelman, I., and Morris, C.T.: *Economic Growth and Social Equity in Developing Countries.* Stanford, Calif.: Stanford University Press, 1973.

Ahluwalia, M. S.: "Income Distribution and Development: Some Stylized Facts." *American Economic Review* 66 (2) (1976), pp. 128-135.

Enke, S.: "Population and Development: A General Model." *Quarterly Journal of Economics* (1963), p. 331-349.

_____: "The Economic Consequences of Rapid Population Growth." *Economic Journal* 81 (1971), pp. 800-811.

Gregory, P., Compbell, J., and Cheny, B.: "A Cost Inclusive Simultaneous Equation Model of Birth Rates." *Econometrica* 40 (2) (1972), pp. 188-201.

Leibenstein, H.: *Economic Backwardness and Economic Growth.* New York: Wiley, 1957.

Lewis, A.: "Economic Development with Unlimited Supplies of Labour." *Manchester School of Economic and Social Studies* 22 (1954), pp. 400-499.

Shultz, T.W.: "Value of the Children." *Journal of Political Economy* 81 (2) (1973), p. 13 (Supplement).

Standing, G.: *Labour Force Participation and Economic Development.* Geneva: ILO, 1978.

Van Ginnneken, W.: *Characteristics of the Head of the Household and Income Inequality: Mexico.* Geneva: ILO, 1975.

Weintraub, R.: "The Birth Rate and Economic Development: An Empirical Study." *Econometrica* 30 (4) (1962), pp. 812-817.

PART TWO

Measurements of Wage and Income Differentials

4

Economic Inequality in
Jordan, 1973-1986

Radwan Ali Sha'ban

1. Introduction

Since 1974, Jordan's economy has experienced a dramatic change in its fortune with a spectacular boom in the period 1974-1982 and a severe recession since 1982. The World Bank's *World Development Report, 1985* listed Jordan as the country with the highest growth rate in real gross domestic product (GDP) for the decade 1973-1983. The compounded average real growth rate of real GDP was 9.4% for the period 1974-1982, whereas it was a mere 2.1% for the period between 1982 and 1986. Given an estimated population growth rate of 3.9% per annum, the per capita real GDP increased by 5.5% per annum during the period 1974-1982, whereas it declined by an average of 1.6% per annum in the period 1982-1986. [1]

This chapter attempts to address the following questions: What were the implications of this phenomenal episode of boom and recession for inequality in Jordan; and were the economic benefits and losses of the boom and recession evenly distributed across different population groups? A subsidiary concern is to analyze interregional and intersectoral inequality and how this evolved during the period under consideration.

Analysis of inequality is quite demanding in terms of data requirement. The usual analysis of income distribution relies on household-level surveys, standard national income accounts being insufficient for the analysis. Unfortunately, it is not possible to trace inequality in Jordan for every year of the period 1973-1986, as only two nationally representative budget surveys were undertaken in Jordan during this period, that is, in 1980 and 1986. The current analysis therefore must rely on these two surveys.

This analysis can be supplemented by the findings of Assaf (1979) for the year 1973. [2] These findings are summarized in Table 4.1 and will be used as a benchmark against which inequality in later years will be compared. Assaf reported a Gini coefficient of 0.4114 for the urban sector

TABLE 4.1
Gini Coefficients of Household Income Inequality, 1973

Area	Gini Coefficient	Average Income [a]
Urban	0.4214	572
Amman	0.4252	603
Irbid	0.4484	561
Balqa	0.3196	428
Karak	0.2354	333
Ma'an	0.3595	487
Rural	0.3280	362
Amman	0.2833	381
Irbid	0.3505	373
Balqa	0.5162	308
Karak	0.2479	291
Ma'an	0.2463	276

[a] Average income is measured in 1973 dinars. Income here refers to "factor income," which consists of wages and salaries, self-employed income and capital income. This concept excludes transfers such as gifts and remittances. Gini coefficient of the more comprehensive "personal income" is 0.4114 for the urban sector and 0.3435 for the rural sector. Unfortunately, the regional breakdown of the more comprehensive "personal income" is not provided in that study.

Source: Assaf (1979), pp. 3-26, 3-33, 3-65, 3-66.

and 0.3435 for the rural sector. Interestingly, Table 4.1 shows that the richer urban regions are more inegalitarian than the poorer ones; Amman and Irbid are the richest and most inegalitarian regions, followed by Ma'an, Balqa, and then Karak. Rural inequality is highest in Balqa, followed by Irbid, Amman, Karak, and Ma'an.

2. Inequality Measurement

The most acceptable criterion for inequality comparison is the Lorenz criterion. A Lorenz curve of income distribution depicts the cumulative fraction of income as a function of the cumulative fraction of the population, arranged in order of increasing income. If all households earn identical income, the Lorenz curve is the diagonal line OB in Figure 4.1; this line is termed the Lorenz curve of "perfect equality." If one person earns all the income in a given economy and everybody else earns zero income, this situation of "perfect inequality" is characterized by the Lorenz curve OAB in Figure 4.1. A Lorenz curve usually lies between these two extremes. The closer it is to the diagonal, the more equitable the distribution is. The Lorenz

FIGURE 4.1
Lorenz Curve

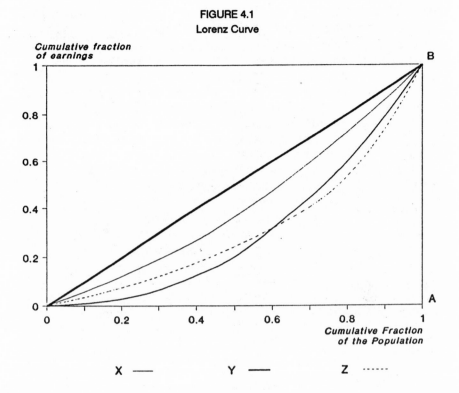

X ———   Y ———   Z ······

criterion of ranking income distributions states that if a Lorenz curve X is closer to the diagonal than Lorenz curve Y and the two curves do not intersect, then distributiom X is more equitable than distribution Y (Figure 4.1). If however, two Lorenz curves cross as those of Y and Z, then the Lorenz criterion cannot make any comparison between the two distributions. Hence, the Lorenz criterion is incomplete and is useful only when the Lorenz curves of the two distributions do not cross. Nonetheless, the Lorenz criterion is quite powerful as it has been shown to be exactly equivalent to a set of "reasonable axioms" regarding equity and to a comparison of distributions based on a general class of reasonable social welfare functions. [3]

To remedy the incompleteness of the Lorenz criterion, researchers usually use a set of measures that are complete in the sense of comparing any two distributions. These measures are usually drawn from Lorenz-consistent measures and should give the same ranking to two distributions as that of the Lorenz criterion whenever the latter can rank these two distributions. Four such complete and Lorenz-consistent measures that are used in this analysis are the Gini coefficient (G), the coefficient of variation (V), Theil (T) index, and Theil (L) index.

The following terms are used in defining these measures.

$$y = (y_1, y_2, y_3, ..., y_N) \text{ is the vector of a given income}$$
distribution of N persons or households.

$r(y_i)$ = rank of person with income y_i, so that the poorest person has a rank of 1 and the richest person has a rank of N.

$Cov(x_1, x_2)$ = covariance of the two variables x_1 and x_2

Y = total income = $\Sigma_i y_i$ (or $\Sigma_i \Sigma_j y_{ij}$)

μ = average income = Y/N

σ = standard deviation = $[(1/N) \Sigma_i (y_i - \mu)^2]^{0.5}$

y_{ij} = income of individual i in population subgroup j

μ_j = average income of population subgroup j

Y_j = total income of population subgroup j

n_j = the number of population subgroup j

The formulae for G, V, T, and L follow:

$$G = 2 \frac{Cov[y_i, r(y_i)]}{Y} \tag{1}$$

$$V = \frac{\sigma}{\mu} \tag{2}$$

$$T = \Sigma_i \Sigma_j \frac{y_{ij}}{Y} \ln\left(\frac{y_{ij}N}{Y}\right) \tag{3}$$

$$= \Sigma_j \left(\frac{Y_j}{Y}\right) T_j + \Sigma_j \left(\frac{Y_j}{Y}\right) \ln\left(\frac{\mu_j}{\mu}\right) \tag{3a}$$

$$L = \Sigma_i \Sigma_j \left(\frac{1}{N}\right) \ln\left(\frac{Y}{y_{ij}N}\right) \tag{4}$$

$$= \Sigma_j \left(\frac{n_j}{N}\right) L_j + \Sigma_j \left(\frac{n_j}{N}\right) \ln\left(\frac{\mu}{\mu_j}\right) \tag{4a}$$

where T_j and L_j are the Theil T and Theil L indices for the population subgroup j, respectively.

The Gini coefficient is the most commonly used measure of inequality. The simplest motivation for its use is that it equals twice the area between the Lorenz curve and the diagonal line of perfect equality. The greater this area is, the more inequitable the distribution is. Thus, a higher value of the Gini coefficient indicates a higher level of inequality. The Gini coefficient ranges between zero, for perfect equality, and one, for perfect inequality. The coefficient of variation is simply defined as the standard deviation divided by the mean of a given distribution and is fairly simple to compute.

Both Theil T and Theil L inequality indices are based on the theory of information. The information content of a given event is negatively related to the probability of occurrence of this event. The expected information of a set of events is mapped onto an index of inequality. The economic intuitive appeal of these indices is at best dismal. Nevertheless, their usefulness arises from the fact that they are the only Lorenz-consistent measure that allow the additive decomposition of overall inequality into a term reflecting inequality within population subgroups and a second term reflecting inequality among these subgroups (see equations 3a and 4a). In the context of the current analysis, these indices permit the estimation of interregional inequality in Jordan.

Insofar as Lorenz curves rank the distributions unequivocally, the four complete measures should also give the same ranking. If the Lorenz curves cross, however, then the four measures may conflict in their inequality ranking because they weight the different positions of the income distribution differently. The coefficient of variation is sensitive to outliers at both ends of the income distribution. The Theil T index is more sensitive to transfers at the richer end of the distribution, whereas the Theil L index is more sensitive to transfers at the lower end of the distribution. The Gini coefficient weights only the differences in the areas between the Lorenz curves without any regard to the position of these areas. Thus, the four measures constitute a good set of inequality indices embodied within different ethical judgments. Furthermore, the Theil indices are useful for analyzing the decomposition of inequality into interregional and intraregional components.

3. Data and Variables

This chapter focuses on three years for the analysis of inequality: 1973, 1980, and 1986. Data from the first year allow an analysis of inequality before the spectacular boom of the late 1970s, whereas the years 1980 and 1986 permit an analysis of inequality in the midst of boom and recession, respectively.

The raw data for the year 1973 used in Assaf's (1979) study are inaccessible to me and are probably "lost." Hence, for the current study I shall rely on Assaf's findings for that year, these findings being summarized in Table 4.1. This chapter focuses more on the analysis of inequality for the years 1980 and 1986. This analysis relies on the two nationally representative budget surveys for these years. Both of these surveys covered only Jordanian households, and single-member households were excluded.

The 1980 Family Expenditure Survey collected information from 1,742 households spanning thirty urban and rural population clusters across Jordan's five governorates. Each household was visited four times, and information was collected about demographic characteristics of household members, daily food expenditure aggregated during the week, monthly expenditure on nonfood items such as clothing and shoes, half-yearly expenditure on durable goods, and annual property, income, and education tax. Initial attempts to collect income data were abandoned.[4]

Questions about the reliability of the 1980 Expenditure Survey were raised in a study produced by the Royal Scientific Society (1985). A thorough investigation of the internal consistency of the data revealed serious inaccuracies and inconsistencies. Corrections to the data were made on the basis of the nature of inconsistency. The nature of data inconsistency included the following:

1. The family size might have fluctuated widely across the four cycles. Family size data were corrected for 166 households.
2. Monthly rental data collected in relation to housing characteristics were sometimes inconsistent with annual data collected in relation to monthly expenditure. Rental data for 44 households were corrected.
3. The quantity and value figures could be inconsistent with each other. Three hundred ninety-five records were corrected for inconsistencies between the quantity and expenditure figures for a given item.
4. Eleven miscellaneous records were corrected for misclassification of data and repeated records.

Another problem of the data set was that food expenditure data were missing in some quarters for certain households. This was taken as an indication that no such data were collected from the concerned households. Thus, food expenditure data were scaled up for these households by proportioning the available quarterly food expenditure data. Eight households were deleted from the sample because of the unavailability of any food data for them. This reduced the sample size to 1,734.

The extent of these data errors threw a justifiable doubt on any conclusions based on this survey. The process of data correction relied on consulting the available computerized files, and this process could have generated biases of its own. Nonetheless, my opinion is that the corrected 1980 Expenditure Survey is more reliable than the raw data set, and the former may be used, albeit cautiously.

In contrast, the 1986 Expenditure Survey was very reliable and consistent. The Department of Statistics did a thorough job in checking and cleaning this data set. The 1986 Expenditure and Income Survey was conducted between March 1986 and February 1987. Data were collected from 2,327 households living in twenty urban and thirty rural population clusters in Jordan's five governorates.[5] The questionnaire sought to collect information regarding the following.

- Housing characteristics: These data were collected at the beginning of the survey.
- Household member characteristics, including age-sex composition and labor market characteristics: These data were collected at the beginning of the survey and were updated after six months and in the last quarter of the survey.
- Sources of household members' income: These data were collected twice for each of the first and last six months of the survey.
- Detailed food expenditure: Data covering 203 commodities were collected for one week in each quarter of the survey period. The information was recorded for each day of the selected week.
- Nonfood expenditure: Data covering 237 commodities were collected four times during the survey four quarters. This expenditure was recorded for each of the months under consideration.

The level of detail and rigor in the 1986 expenditure survey was much better than that of the 1980 survey. Furthermore, the 1986 survey sought to collect information on household sources of income. Thus, the analysis of the 1986 survey will focus on both expenditure and income.

This raises the issue as to what the appropriate indicator of household welfare may be. It is often argued that consumption expenditure is a better measure of economic welfare than is income. This argument is based on the permanent income hypothesis, which argues that consumption expenditure is usually based on the long-term expected income and will thus be subject to smaller fluctuations than actual income. Also, it can be argued that consumption expenditure is a measure of people's actual welfare, whereas income measures people's potential welfare. The analysis of expenditure inequality should also be useful for measuring income inequality; expenditure inequality should be taken as a lower bound for income inequality because richer people usually save a higher proportion of their income. This is indeed the relation between income and expenditure inequality in 1986, as illustrated in section 5.

All of these arguments suggest expenditure to be a better indicator of welfare than income. But in this analysis, the data availability is a limiting factor: Assaf's inequality analysis for 1973 relied solely on income data; the current analysis of inequality in 1980 is based only on expenditure data; and the analysis of inequality for 1986 is based on both income and expenditure data.

4. 1980 Expenditure Inequality

The analysis of inequality in 1980 relies on household expenditure data, as income data are not available. Table 4.2 provides the estimates of four complete inequality measures, (Gini coefficient, coefficient of variation, Theil T index and Theil L index), as well as the average household income and sample size. The analysis is carried out both for the country as a whole and for the urban and rural sectors with a breakdown at the regional level of Jordan's five governorates. Figure 4.2 illustrates the Lorenz curves for the rural sector of the five governorates. The average household expenditure in Table 4.2 is 2,863 dinars per annum. Given an average household size of 7.17, this implies an average annual per capita

TABLE 4.2
Household Expenditure Inequality, 1980

Area	Gini Coefficient	Coefficient of Variation	Theil T Index	Theil L Index	Average (JD)	Sample Size
Total	0.389	0.840	0.263	0.256	2,862.85	1,734
Urban	0.380	0.817	0.250	0.244	3,046.37	1,453
Amman	0.370	0.771	0.233	0.231	3,395.10	959
Irbid	0.375	0.822	0.247	0.238	2,374.67	306
Balqa	0.417	1.045	0.330	0.298	3,018.84	76
Karak	0.261	0.512	0.114	0.116	1,842.02	46
Ma'an	0.266	0.528	0.118	0.115	1,964.61	66
Rural	0.380	0.851	0.255	0.238	1,913.88	281
Amman	0.480	1.093	0.392	0.356	2,920.12	23
Irbid	0.369	0.750	0.226	0.232	2,193.93	134
Balqa	0.302	0.522	0.130	0.143	1,624.67	23
Karak	0.297	0.586	0.143	0.135	1,440.46	58
Ma'an	0.325	0.732	0.191	0.175	1,296.21	43
Between			0.029	0.033		
% Between			11.5	12.9		

Source: Department of Statistics, Family Expenditure Survey, 1986 (unpublished 1988 draft).

expenditure of 399 dinars in 1980. This is comparable to the national accounting statistics, in which the per capita gross domestic product is given at 444 dinars.

The Gini coefficients of expenditure inequality for 1980 given in Table 4.2 are comparable to those of income inequality in 1973 given in Table 4.1. Nevertheless, given that expenditure inequality tends to be smaller than income inequality, we can argue that inequality in 1980 tended to be slightly higher than 1973.

The more important point is the sectoral aspect of the change in inequality. Although the overall Gini coefficient seemed to be stable for the whole urban sector for the period 1973-1980, rural inequality undoubtedly increased during the same period. The Gini coefficient for the rural household incomes was 0.328 in 1973, whereas it was 0.380 for rural household expenditure in 1980. This dramatic increase in rural inequality occurred simultaneously with impressive rates of growth in agricultural output.

FIGURE 4.2
Lorenz Curves of Household Expenditure, 1980
Rural Sector

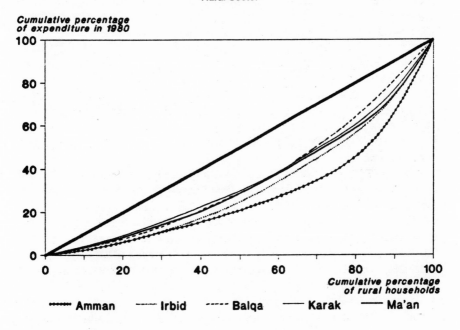

Cumulative percentage
of expenditure in 1980

****** Amman   ------ Irbid   ----- Balqa   ——— Karak   ——— Ma'an

Cumulative percentage
of rural households

The Lorenz curves of rural inequality are presented in Figure 4.2. It clearly illustrates that the Amman governorate has the most inequitable rural sector. In fact, the level of rural inequality in Amman is much higher than in other governorates. This can partially be explained by the dramatic increase in urban land value that took place in the late 1970s and spilled over into Amman's rural areas more than it did into other rural areas. This increase would exacerbate the existing wealth inequality and be reflected in expenditure inequality. Furthermore, an increasing number of richer households took to living in Amman's outlying rural areas as the boundaries of Amman's metropolitan area expanded, as can be seen by the relatively high average household expenditure in Amman's rural area listed in Table 4.2.

Figure 4.2 demonstrates that Irbid is the second ranking governorate in terms of rural inequality after Amman. The Lorenz curves for household expenditure in the rural sector of Balqa, Karak, and Ma'an cross each other. Nevertheless, the four indices of inequality in Table 4.2 show that Ma'an's rural inequality is greater than that of Balqa and Karak.

Concerning interregional urban inequality, the Lorenz curve illustrates that the five governorates can be divided into three groups on the count of household expenditure inequality. The urban sector of Balqa is the most inegalitarian, as its Lorenz curve is farthest away from the diagonal. Amman and Irbid have an intermediate level of inequality, although Irbid is slightly more inequitable. Karak and Ma'an fall in the most equitable group. The Lorenz curves of Karak and Ma'an cross, so we cannot rank inequality in these two regions absolutely. Indeed, Ma'an is ranked to be more inequitable by the Gini coefficient, the coefficient of variation, and the Theil T index; but the Theil L index gives the opposite ranking. This is to be expected because the Theil L index is more sensitive at the lower end of the distribution.

The Theil T and L indices provide an additive decomposability of overall inequality in Jordan. If Jordan is divided into ten groups reflecting the rural and urban areas of its five governorates, then in 1980 close to 88% of the overall inequality was a result of inequality within these ten groups, and only about 12% of the overall inequality was a reflection of interregional inequality. This is indeed a useful result as it suggests that to reduce overall inequality, more attention must be given to intraregional inequality than to interregional inequality.

In order to analyze the impact of the tax system on inequality, two Lorenz curves were drawn together—one for total expenditure including taxes, and the other for household expenditure excluding taxes. These reflect "pretax" and "posttax" expenditure. The two Lorenz curves are practically superimposed. Thus, we can conclude that the direct (income, property, and education) tax system does not essentially alter equality. This should come as no surprise because Jordan's fiscal system relies more heavily on indirect taxation for its revenues.

5. 1986 Expenditure and Income Inequality

Because the 1986 survey included data on both expenditure and income, inequality was analyzed using both variables for that year. Some households did not provide data for every stage of the survey. The expenditure data for these households were scaled up by seasonally adjusted factors to give annual figures for food and nonfood expenditure, which were then added to give the total household expenditure. Rates of total household expenditure were thus available for 2,325 households.

Income data were collected twice in the survey year. If income data were missing for either stage of the income survey, the household in question was deleted from the income analysis. Thus, the total number of households providing complete income data was 2,236. The household income includes wages and salaries; income of the self-employed; retirement income; income from ownership of commercial, industrial, service, or agricultural enterprises; rent income; interest and dividends; and remittance income. The sale of land and property was considered an income item for the purposes of the survey but is not included in the definition of income used here because it reflects a portfolio adjustment on the part of the household, not an increase in wealth. The incomes of all members of the household were added to arrive at the total household income.

It is interesting to observe that in 1986 the average household income was JD 3,055, and the average household expenditure was JD 3,831. This does not indicate a negative saving rate of 25% but rather the tendency on the part of households to underestimate their income, perhaps for fear of tax authorities, and to overestimate their expenditure, possibly for reasons of social prestige. Although this underestimation of income and overestimation of expenditure may bias the measures of inequality, this bias is probably minimal if we assume that the underestimation and overestimation do not correlate with income or expenditure. There is no reason to assume that such a correlation is significant.

Figures 4.3 and 4.4 illustrate the regional Lorenz curve of household expenditure for the urban and rural sectors, respectively. The estimates of the complete household inequality measures are given in Table 4.3. The striking datum in Table 4.3 is that inequality was quite low in 1986. The overall Gini coefficient was 0.346, as compared with a coefficient 0.389 in 1980. This represents a noticeable increase in equity in Jordan during such a short period and implies that on average and relatively speaking, rich people were more affected by the mid-1980s recession than poor people were. This increase in equity can be partially explained by Had-

FIGURE 4.3
Lorenz Curves of Household Expenditure, 1986
Urban Sector

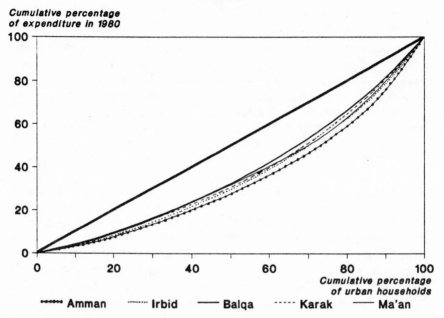

*Cumulative percentage
of expenditure in 1980*

dad's (1988) finding that the share of wages and salaries in GDP increased in the period 1980-1986.

When we make a comparison of urban expenditure inequality by region, we find that Balqa is the most egalitarian urban region and Amman the most inegalitarian. The Lorenz curves of the three remaining regions-- Irbid, Karak, and Ma'an--are fairly close to each other. But the four measures of inequality in Table 4.3 agree on ranking Ma'an to be more equitable than Karak, which in turn is more equitable than Irbid.

As shown in Figure 4.4, the Lorenz curves of rural expenditure inequality in the five regions cross, and a clear absolute ranking is not possible. Here we should turn to Table 4.3 to find that the four inequality measures agree on ranking Ma'an as the most equitable rural region and Irbid as the most inequitable rural region. The ranking of the other three regions depends on the measure used and the bias implicit in that measure.

When we turn to income inequality (Table 4.4), we find that it is greater

FIGURE 4.4
Lorenz Curves of Household Expenditure, 1986
Rural Sector

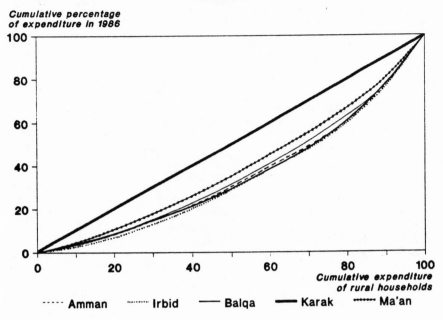

*Cumulative percentage
of expenditure in 1986*

----- Amman   ········ Irbid   ——— Balqa   ▬▬▬ Karak   ······· Ma'an

than expenditure inequality, as expected. This is true not only at the national level but also at the sectoral level and at the regional level for each sector. This finding supports the hypothesis that richer people tend to save a higher proportion of their income than do poorer people. When we compare income inequality in 1986 with that in 1973 we find that the overall Gini coefficient for the urban sector declined from 0.4114 in 1973 to 0.3923 in 1986, while the overall rural Gini coefficient increased from 0.3435 to 0.3776 during the same period.

In terms of regional ranking, Table 4.4 suggests that urban income is most equitable in Irbid and least equitable in Amman. The Lorenz curves for Balqa, Karak, and Ma'an cross each other, and the four inequality measures provide conflicting rankings. As for rural incomes, Ma'an is clearly the most egalitarian region. Amman and Irbid are the most inegalitarian regions in terms of rural income. Their Lorenz curves cross twice and illustrate that the richest group in Irbid is relatively better off than that

TABLE 4.3
Household Expenditure Inequality, 1986

Area	Gini Coefficient	Coefficient of Variation	Theil T Index	Theil L Index	Average (JD)	Sample Size
Total	0.346	0.744	0.210	0.205	3,831.2	2,325
Urban	0.343	0.727	0.204	0.200	4,213.3	1,590
Amman	0.332	0.695	0.189	0.185	4,727.1	1,189
Irbid	0.292	0.565	0.139	0.142	2,747.8	183
Balqa	0.252	0.461	0.104	0.119	2,715.9	109
Karak	0.278	0.515	0.119	0.121	3,170.5	52
Ma'an	0.273	0.502	0.116	0.120	2,014.9	57
Rural	0.317	0.700	0.182	0.177	3,004.5	735
Amman	0.307	0.691	0.172	0.180	3,402.2	209
Irbid	0.325	0.724	0.194	0.194	2,713.0	352
Balqa	0.290	0.627	0.149	0.141	4,507.3	42
Karak	0.309	0.597	0.151	0.146	2,783.7	60
Ma'an	0.222	0.408	0.078	0.082	2,582.3	72
Between			0.033	0.035		
% Between			15.90	17.20		

Source: Department of Statistics, Family Expenditure Survey, 1986 (unpublished 1988 drafts).

in Amman. It is interesting to see that the coefficient of variation, which is sensitive to outliers at the high end of the distribution, ranks Amman as more equitable then Irbid, whereas the other three measures provide the opposite ranking.

The additive decomposability of the Theil indices allows us to measure the component of interregional inequality in overall inequality. Inequality between the ten rural and urban sectors of the five governorates contributes about 16% to overall expenditure inequality and about 12% to overall income inequality.

6. Conclusions

Instead of summarizing the main results of this chapter, let me focus on one central issue here--namely, the changes in inequality in the period 1973-1986. Two significant points should be borne in mind. First, the methodology of data collection and the concept of income in Assaf's study for 1973 were different from those of the Family Expenditure and Income Survey for 1986. Second, the inequality measures for 1980 should be treated with caution because of the inaccuracies in the 1980 Family

TABLE 4.4
Household Income Inequality, 1986

Area	Gini Coefficient	Coefficient of Variation	Theil T Index	Theil L Index	Average (JD)	Sample Size
Total	0.3972	0.9815	0.295	0.272	3,054.6	2,236
Urban	0.3923	0.9200	0.280	0.266	3,362.9	1,511
Amman	0.3827	0.8994	0.267	0.246	3,759.7	1,120
Irbid	0.3277	0.6476	0.176	0.175	2,617.0	180
Balqa	0.3611	0.6825	0.215	0.277	1,721.2	105
Karak	0.3657	0.7592	0.223	0.208	2,332.3	51
Ma'an	0.3650	0.7226	0.222	0.231	1,811.8	55
Rural	0.3776	1.1110	0.295	0.247	2,412.0	725
Amman	0.4146	0.9650	0.313	0.283	2,944.7	205
Irbid	0.3670	1.2975	0.311	0.241	2,358.0	347
Balqa	0.3179	0.5797	0.152	0.156	2,333.1	42
Karak	0.3052	0.5660	0.151	0.176	1,524.2	59
Ma'an	0.2810	0.5182	0.123	0.129	1,928.9	72
Between			0.033	0.036		
% Between			11.30	13.30		

Source: Department of Statistics, *Family Expenditure Survey, 1986* (unpublished 1988 draft).

Expenditure Survey, despite the thorough corrections undertaken for the purposes of this chapter.

Figure 4.5 illustrates the overall Lorenz curves for four variables: income in 1973, expenditure in 1980, expenditure in 1986, and income in 1986. That the expenditure distribution is more equitable than the income distribution in 1986 supports the contention that expenditure inequality can be taken as a lower bound for income inequality.

Figure 4.5 also illustrates that expenditure inequality declined between 1980 and 1986, indicating that overall inequality declined during this period. When we move to the earlier period, it is difficult to make the comparison because we only have income data for 1973 and expenditure data for 1980. The Lorenz curves of these two categories cross each other. Assuming the relation between the Lorenz curves of income and expenditure for 1980 to be similar to that for 1986, I construct a hypothetical Lorenz curve for income distribution in 1980. This curve is shown in Figure 4.5. This hypothetical Lorenz curve for income in 1980 crosses the Lorenz curve for income in 1973. Nevertheless, the lower and middle classes were better off in 1973, indicating that an inequality index that is biased toward the lower classes will indicate increasing inequality between the

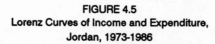

FIGURE 4.5
Lorenz Curves of Income and Expenditure,
Jordan, 1973-1986

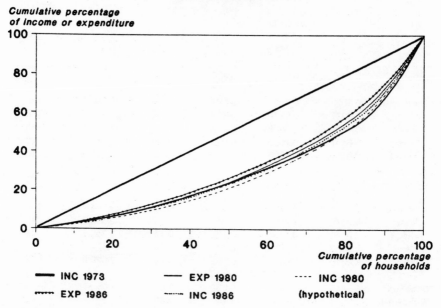

years 1973 and 1980.

A more important point is the evolution of sectoral inequality. Although it seems that urban inequality remained relatively unchanged in the period 1973-1980, inequality declined in the period 1980-1986. Urban household income inequality was less in 1986 than in 1973. When we turn to rural household inequality, we can see that inequality increased in the period 1973-1980, and although it declined between 1980 and 1986, the level of rural household income inequality was still higher in 1986 than in 1973.

Notes

The author wishes to acknowledge the support of Jordan's Ministry of Planning and financial support from the Joint Committee on the Near and Middle East of the American Council of Learned Societies and the Social Science Research Council. Competent research assistance was provided by Patricio Arrau, Shen-Yuan

Chien, and Mohammad Al-Anzi.

1. For a more detailed discussion of the pattern of growth, see Radwan Ali Sha'ban: *The Distribution of Economic Welfare in Jordan* (forthcoming), Chap. 1. The figures are based on data from various annual bulletins of the Central Bank of Jordan.

2. Assaf's (1979) unpublished study is the only existing study based on household-level data; it dealt with the topic of inequality in Jordan.

3. See Sha'ban (forthcoming) and Anand (1983) for an exact statement of equivalence of the Lorenz criterion, a set of reasonable axioms regarding equity, and a social welfare function approach to comparison of distributions.

4. People are generally afraid that income data may be used to catch tax evaders.

5. The sample design was such that the data were representative of the five governorates; the design was not changed when the regional boundaries were redrawn in 1986 to allow for eight governorates. Thus, the current analysis uses the five-governorate classification. This should also make it easy to compare the results of this analysis with those of 1973 and 1980.

References and Bibliography

Anand, S.: *Inequality and Poverty in Malaysia: Measurement and Decomposition.* New York: Oxford University Press, 1983.

Assaf, G.: *The Size Distribution of Income in Jordan in 1973.* Amman: Royal Scientific Society, 1979, draft.

Atkinson, A.B.: "On Measurement of Inequality." *Journal of Economic Theory* 2 (3) (1970).

_____: "The Economics of Inequality." Oxford: Claredon Press, 1975.

Dasgupta, P., Sen, A.K., and Starrett, D.: "Notes on the Measurement of Inequality." *Journal of Economic Theory* 6 (2) (1973).

Department of Statistics: *Family Expenditure Survey, 1980.* Amman, n.d.

_____: *Family Expenditure Survey, 1986.* Amman, unpublished 1988 draft.

Fields, G.S.: *Poverty, Inequality and Development.* New York: Cambridge University Press, 1980.

Foster, J.E.: "Economic Poverty: A Survey of Aggregate Measures."*Advances in Econometrics* 3 (1984).

_____: "Inequality Measurement." Young, H. Peyton (ed.): *Fair Allocations, American Mathematical Society Proceedings of Symposia in Applied Mathematics* 33, 1985.

Glewwe, P.: "The Distribution of Income in Sri Lanka in 1969-70 and 1980-81: A Decomposition Analysis." *Journal of Development Economics* (1978).

Haddad, A.: "Jordan's Income Distribution in Retrospect." Amman, 1988, draft (see Chapter 2).

Paukert, F.: "Income Distribution at Different Levels of Development." *International Labor Review* (August-September 1973).

Radwan, S.: *Agrarian Reform and Rural Poverty, Egypt, 1952-1975.* Geneva: ILO, 1977.

Royal Scientific Society: "Demand Analysis in Jordan." Amman: Royal Scientific

Society, 1985.

Sen, A.: *Poverty and Famines: An Essay on Entitlement and Deprivation.* Oxford: Oxford University Press, 1984.

Sha'ban, R.A.: *The Distribution of Economic Welfare in Jordan.* Forthcoming.

World Bank: *Jordan: Efficiency and Equity of Government Revenues and Social Expenditures.* Washington, D.C.: World Bank, Report 5697-JO, 1985.

_____: Jordan: *Issues of Employment and Labour Market Imbalances.* 2 Vols. Washington, D.C.: World Bank, Report 5117-JO, 1986.

_____: *World Development Report, 1985.* New York: Oxford University Press, 1985.

5

Wage Distribution Among Private Sector Workers Subject to Social Security Regulations

Saleh Al-Khasawneh

1. Introduction

Wages are defined as the cost of labor or the returns of labor. Hence, they are considered to be one of the constituents of production costs and are reflected in productivity and in the competitiveness of producers inside as well as outside the national economy. Wages also constitute a source of income, amounting in Jordan to at least 40% of the gross domestic product (GDP) throughout the period 1981-1986, as is shown in Table 5.1.

The importance of wages and their effect on such factors as production costs, price levels, inflation, levels of employment and unemployment, the volume of the GDP, the patterns of income and wealth distribution, and the poverty line in a given society have earned them the attention of decision-

TABLE 5.1
Wages as a Percentage of GDP, 1981-1987 (million JD)

Year	GDP	Wages	Wages (%)
1981	1164.2	474.1	40.72
1982	1321.2	550.3	41.65
1983	1422.7	604.4	42.50
1984	1498.4	649.8	43.37
1985	1605.0	706.3	43.98
1986	1639.9	759.5	46.31
1987	1686.3	783.1	46.44

Source: CBJ Monthly Statistical Bulletin 24 (8) (August 1988),Table 47.

makers, economists, and business people. This chapter sheds some light on the 1987 pattern of the wage bill in Jordan's private sector.

1.1 Objectives

The aim of this chapter is to analyze some particular characteristics of wages and salaries in the private sector. Specifically, this chapter analyzes the averages and levels of wage distribution among both Jordanian and non-Jordanian workers who are subject to social security regulations. The levels and averages of wages are divided into categories and classified by economic sector, professional level, sex, geographic distribution, age, marital status,and nationality. The resulting data are then analyzed according to these categories and classifications.

1.2 Scope

As mentioned, this chapter covers all workers subject to social security regulations at the end of the second quarter of 1987. The grand total of affiliated workers at the time was 398,458, which amounted to 60% of the total labor force in the local market in both the private and public sectors, or 95% of workers in the private sector. Of these, 262,180 were Jordanian, and the remaining 136,278 were non-Jordanian.

The overall average monthly wage paid to these workers was JD 104, which put the total monthly wage figure at JD 42 million and the annual wage figure at JD 499 million. This constituted 64% of the total of wages paid in the kingdom, which amounted to JD 783 million in 1987.

This chapter uses data related to wages and salaries for workers subject to social security regulations as they appear in the records of the computer department of the Social Security Corporation. These records are considered objective and accurate, especially because they represent financial privileges and commitments for social security subscribers, their employers, and the Social Security Corporation.

The large size of the data sample gives special importance to this chapter, given its subject matter, the distribution of income from wages, and its effects on production costs, productivity, price levels, employment and unemployment levels, and income and wealth distribution patterns. This study is the first of its kind in this field.

1.3 Methodology

This chapter relies solely on data related to wages of all workers subject to social security regulations at the end of the second quarter of 1987. These data are categorized and classified by wage averages against economic activity and profession into eleven equal bands of JD 50 per month. The first band includes wages of less than JD 50, the second comprises wages from JD 50 to JD 100, and so on up to the last band, which covers wages in excess of JD 500 per month. Tables showing the distribution of workers subject to social security regulations at the end of the second quarter of 1987 across these eleven equal wage groups are given in the Appendix to this book.

From these figures, the weighted average wages are calculated for each category by multiplying the median of each subcategory by the frequency (number of workers in that subcategory) and dividing the product by the total number of workers in that category. For the final analysis, these wage averages are used to study the distribution of wages by sector of the economy, profession, and so on as explained in the following sections.

2. Findings

2.1 Income Distribution by Economic Sector

Table 5.2 indicates the distribution of average wages by economic sector. The table shows that the overall average monthly wage of workers subject to social security regulations was JD 104. Hence, the total wages paid to workers subject to social security regulations were 42 million monthly, or JD 499 million annually. This figure can be compared with the total contribution of all wages to the GDP, which amounted to JD 783 million

TABLE 5.2
Average Wages by Economic Activity, 1987 (JD) [a]

Economic Sectors	Jordanians	Non-Jordanians	All Workers
Agriculture, hunting, and forestry	84.580	83.820	84.450
Manufacture, mining, and energy	108.550	87.430	101.440
Wholesale and retail trade	110.470	92.170	104.740
Construction	129.280	109.400	118.390
Storage and transportation	131.930	104.670	122.290
Finance and insurance	141.700	147.280	142.080
Tourism	89.910	91.260	90.500
Other services	108.680	83.770	98.220
Unspecified	98.020	88.660	95.170
All sectors	109.930	93.680	104.370

[a] One Jordanian dinar equals one thousand fils.
In June 1987, one J.D. equalled 2.90 U.S. dollars.

Source: Social Security Corporation, computer section data--provided for the computer center of the Royal Scientific Society at the end of the second quarter of 1987; cumulative affiliated individuals taken as representative for Jordan's private sector labor force.

in 1987.

Table 5.2 also shows that the overall average wage of the Jordanians included in the study (JD 110) was higher than that of the non-Jordanians (JD 93.700). This was the case for average wages in all sectors except finance and tourism.

Wages in finance had the highest average: The wage for all workers in this sector averaged JD 142 monthly. The wage average for non-Jordanians was JD 147.280 monthly, compared with JD 141.700 for Jordanians. An explanation for this difference is that the employment of non-Jordanians in these sectors was limited to a small number (less than 1,000) of highly qualified personnel who earned high salaries. Non-Jordanians employed in this sector earning in excess of JD 500 accounted for 6.29% of non-Jordanians as opposed to 2.33% of Jordanians employed in finance and insurance services. These figures are given in Tables 5A.6 and 5A.7 in the Appendix.

Workers in transportation and storage were the second highest paid, earning on average JD 122.300 (JD 132 for Jordanians and JD 104.700 for non-Jordanians). In third place came construction workers, who earned JD 118.400 (JD 129.300 for Jordanians and JD 109.400 for non-Jordanians). Next came workers in the wholesale and retail sector, where the overall wage average was similar to that in all other sectors, although the discrepancy between wages of Jordanians (JD 110.500) and non-Jordanians (JD 92.200) was larger.

In manufacturing, mining and energy; the service industries; and tourism, average wages (JD 101.400, JD 98.200, and JD 90.500, respectively) were less than the overall average. Nevertheless, the average wage of Jordanian workers was JD 108.600 in manufacturing industries, and JD 108.700 in service industries, that is, greater than the national average. In tourism, where the average wage was JD 90.500, Jordanians earned on average JD 89.900, and non-Jordanians earned JD 91.300. One reason for the higher wages paid to non-Jordanians (numbering 6,101 workers, compared to 7,900 Jordanian workers) may have been the nonavailability of skilled local labor and the consequent hiring of skilled non-Jordanians. This interpretation is backed by the distribution of workers according to wage groups. Table 5A.7 shows that non-Jordanians who earned more than JD 500 accounted for 1.66% of the non-Jordanians in tourism, while Jordanians earning this level of wage accounted for only 0.28% of the total number of Jordanians in tourism (see Table 5A.6). Moreover, non-Jordanians earning in excess of JD 300 amounted to 3.59% while only 1.36% of the Jordanians in tourism belonged to this wage group. The lowest wages paid, averaging JD 84.450, were in agriculture. In this sector, wages of Jordanians, at JD 84.580, were both close to the average and to those of non-Jordanians, at JD 83.800.

The reason for this equivalence is that most agricultural workers are employed by large institutions or landowners who pay reasonable salaries regardless of nationality. Moreover, most agricultural workers who are registered with the Social Security Corporation are Jordanian: 12,129 as opposed to 2,540 non-Jordanians. It is believed that quite a number non-Jordanian agricultural workers are not registered. An inquiry into the overall wages bill and into wage structure of the agricultural sector would be desirable and might reveal deviations in average wages as compared to Table 5.2.

2.2 Wage Distribution by Main Occupation

Table 5.3 looks at wage distribution by main occupation. It shows that the highest wages, on average, went to administrators and administrative staff, who constituted 0.53% of the total work force covered by the sample. On average, members of this category earned JD 324.900: JD 321 for Jordanians and JD 338 for non-Jordanians. This is three times the overall wage average, more in the case of non-Jordanians. These results seem reasonable and acceptable because administrative staff receive higher remuneration, especially expatriates who are brought to Jordan to answer to a pressing need that requires their specializations. A more detailed picture is given in Tables 5A.2, 5A.8, and 5A.9. Managers and administrative staff form a very small fraction of the total sample size. Nevertheless, their representation in the highest wage band (JD 500 and more) is remarkably high. More than one out of four members of this profession earn monthly salaries of JD 500 and more. Less than two out of one hundred members of all the other specified professional groups earn such a wage. This big gap can be explained, in part, by the employment status of highly trained professionals. If they are not working as managers, they

TABLE 5.3
Wage Averages by Main Professional Groups, 1987 (JD)

Main Professional Groups	Jordanians	Non-Jordanians	All Workers
Specialists, technicians	128.780	132.450	129.550
Managers and administrative staff	320.960	338.080	324.860
Clerical staff	114.350	115.840	114.540
Sales persons	128.540	109.200	124.390
Service workers	80.280	67.850	74.800
Agricultural workers	80.490	72.290	77.020
Production-line and transportation workers	100.370	92.160	96.960
Unspecified	150.930	147.060	150.100
Total	109.930	93.680	104.370

Source : Social Security Corporation, computer section.

are frequently working as employers or the self-employed. This is typically the case for lawyers, medical doctors, and architects. Therefore, they do not enter the social security scheme.

Specialists and technicians, who constituted 7.5% of the total labor force covered by the study, were the second highest paid wage group. On average, they received JD 129.600: JD 128.800 for Jordanians and JD 132.500 for non-Jordanians.

The third highest wages were paid to sales staff, who averaged JD 124.400 per month: JD 128.500 for Jordanians and JD 109.200 for non-Jordanians. In fourth place came clerical staff, who averaged JD 114.500. The discrepancy between the wages of Jordanians, JD 114.350, and those of non-Jordanians, JD 115.840, was small. It should be noted that all wages in the aforementioned categories were greater than the overall average.

The lowest wages were earned by workers in production industries, agriculture, and service industries, who constituted 45%, 6%, and 16% of the total work force, respectively and whose wages averaged JD 97, JD 77, and JD 75. All wages in these categories were less than the overall average, although Jordanians' wages were higher than those of non-Jordanians.

It should be noted that 7.7% of the work force subject to social security received less than JD 50 per month; 59% received between JD 50 and JD 100; and 20% received between JD 100 and JD 150. In other words, 67% of the work force receive less than JD 100, while 87% received less than JD 150. Those earning more than JD 200 constituted less than 7% of the total work force covered by the study, while those earning more than JD 300 constituted about 4%. (For calculation of these figures, see the last rows of tables 5A.8 and 5A.9.)

When we look at Jordanian workers only, 5% received less than JD 50, 62% earned less than JD 100, and 84.5% earned less than JD 150. Among non-Jordanians, 12.4% earned less than JD 50, 74.8% earned less than JD 100, and 90.9% earned less than 150, which again shows that non-Jordanians tended to earn less than Jordanians. At the other end of the scale, Jordanians earning more than JD 200 constituted 8% of the total Jordanian work force, while non-Jordanians on a similar wage accounted for 5% of the total non-Jordanian work force covered by the study.

2.3 Wage Distribution by Sex

Table 5.4 shows that the wage average for males was JD 106, as opposed to JD 91.800 for females. These figures have to be compared with the overall average of JD 104.400 per month for all workers covered by the study. Wages of Jordanian males averaged JD 113.600, while those of non-Jordanian males averaged JD 93.200. In contrast, wages of Jordanian females averaged JD 89.600, while those of non-Jordanian females averaged JD 103.300. This gives a clear indication that there is a specific

TABLE 5.4
Wage Averages by Sex, 1987 (JD)

Sex	Jordanians	Non-Jordanians	Total
Males	113.600	93.200	106.140
Females	89.560	103.340	91.760
Total	109.930	93.680	104.370

Source: Social Security Corporation, computer section.

demand for the employment of foreign women with skills that necessitate payment of higher salaries. The characteristics of this demand also could be a possible topic for future research. From the information available (see Table 5A.11 and 5A.3), the average wages and salaries for non-Jordanian females hint at a dual labor market. That is, an above average percentage of non-Jordanian females earn less than JD 50. At the same time, an above average percentage of non-Jordanian females are represented in the wage bands of JD 300 and more. This relation holds true not only with respect to Jordanian females but non-Jordanian males as well.

When we examine the distribution of workers subject to social security regulation according to the wage bands, we see that the majority received between JD 50 and JD 100. Overall, 58.8% of the men and 60% of the women were in this category. Among male workers, this category included 56.3% of the Jordanians and 63% of the non-Jordanians, while among female workers it comprised 62% of the Jordanians and 50% of the non-Jordanians.

The second largest group was workers earning from JD 100 to JD 150. This category covered 20.5% of male workers and 17% of female workers. Of males, 23% of the Jordanians were in this category, as were 16% of the non-Jordanians, while among females, 16.8% of the Jordanians were in this group, as were 18% of the non-Jordanians.

The proportion of men earning less then JD 50 was 7%, as opposed to 12.9% of women. Among Jordanian males the proportion is as low as 4%, but it stands at 12.3% among non-Jordanians. Among females it stood at 12.6% for Jordanians and 14.4% for non-Jordanians.

These figures show that 65% of the males included in the study received less than JD 100 (60% of the Jordanians and 75% of the non-Jordanians) compared with 73% of the females (74.5% of the Jordanians and 64% of the non-Jordanians). Moreover, 85% of the males and 90% of the females received less than JD 150. The greater than JD 200 wage bracket included only 8% of the males--9% of the Jordanians and 5% of the non-Jordanians-- and 4.2% of the females--3.6% of the Jordanians and 8% of the non-Jordanians.

It can be seen from the preceding data that average wages were higher for males than for females. Among Jordanians there was a higher concentration of the females in low income brackets (less than JD 100) than there was of the males. In contrast, among non-Jordanians there was a higher concentration of the males than of the females in the same category. This was true despite the dual nature of the labor demand for non-Jordanian females. The high concentration of non-Jordanian males in the lowest bands dominated in this respect.

2.4 Wage Distribution by Governorate

The sample data follow the old administrative structure of Jordan with five governorates on the East Bank and three governorates on the West Bank. In 1987, 2,419 residents from the West Bank were subject to social security in Jordan. This amounted to less than 1% of the total number of workers in the sample. The obvious reason for such a low social security coverage was the ongoing Arab-Israeli conflict, which led to the Israeli occupation of the West Bank in 1967. Since then, the governorates of Jerusalem, Hebron, and Nablus have been cut off from many East Bank activities. In this context it should be noted that at the end of July 1988, Jordan severed all legal and administrative links with the Occupied Territories.

Before we turn to the five remaining East Bank governorates, let me briefly state some information on the West Bank workers subject to social security in Jordan. According to Table 5A.4, most of them came from the Jerusalem and Nablus governorates. Their wages were less than the Jordanian average, particularly in Nablus and Hebron governorates. In fact, 93% of the enrolled workers of the West Bank earned less than JD 150. Of course, the data should not be misinterpreted because the sample did not seem to represent the West Bank work force appropriately (see Chapter 7).

Of the five East Bank governorates, Amman is by far the largest in terms of size and labor force. It includes the city of Zarqa and Greater Amman Municipality. More than half of Jordan's population is concentrated in Amman governorate. According to Table 5A.4, Irbid comes next in terms of size of labor force, followed by Ma'an and Karak. Balqa governorate comes last both in labor and level of wages.

Table 5.5 shows that the highest wages were paid in Karak, where the average was JD 113.600, compared with the national average of JD 104.400. The average wage for non-Jordanians was higher (JD 120.500) than that of Jordanians (JD 110.800). This was due to the presence in Karak of large enterprises such as the potash mines and Al-Hasa phosphate mines. These companies paid high salaries to attract workers to their

TABLE 5.5
Wage Distribution of Workers According to Governorates, 1987 (JD)

Governorate	Jordanians	Non-Jordanians	Average
Amman	113.070	92.330	106.130
Jerusalem	97.260	112.500	97.830
Irbid	96.580	97.000	96.690
Nablus	89.430	93.140	89.150
Hebron	85.470	95.590	85.920
Balqa	91.770	92.780	92.050
Karak	110.750	120.510	113.640
Ma'an	107.590	91.480	99.360
Undeclared	92.830	82.780	88.550
General wage average	109.930	93.680	104.370

Source: Social Security Corporation, computer section.

sites, especially highly qualified non-Jordanians whose specializations were not available locally.

The second highest paying governorate was Amman, which had the highest concentration of labor. The average salary there was JD 106.100 (JD 113 for Jordanians and JD 92.300 for non-Jordanians), which was very close to the national average of JD 104.

Third came Ma'an, which also housed some large enterprises such as the South Cement Company, glass and fertilizer factories, and Al-Shidieh phosphate mine. The average wage was JD 99.400 (JD 107.600 for Jordanians and JD 91.500 for non-Jordanians). In Irbid and Balqa governorates, the average wages were JD 96.700 and JD 92, respectively. Wages were slightly higher for non-Jordanian labor.

The low level of wages both in Irbid and Balqa governorates most likely was due to the combined effect of rural bias (see Chapter 4 on rural-urban income differentials) and predominance of small-scale industries. In the absence of large-scale enterprises such as phosphate mines, the wage bill of Irbid and Balqa governorates was stuck at a less than average level. Further research is required, however, to substantiate this conjecture.

2.5 Wage Distribution by Age Group

When calculating average wages and salaries by age groups, we would expect a steady increase of wage levels with increasing age until age came close to retirement. In fact, the well-known life cycle income hypothesis is illustrated by an inverted U-shaped curve with "income" along the vertical and "age" along the horizontal axis. In Jordan, the typical age of entry to the labor market is seventeen because a high number of Jordanians take twelve years of schooling. The legal retirement age is sixty for men and fifty-five for women.

Table 5.6 shows wages to be markedly lower in the three lowest age brackets--less than seventeen years, seventeen to twenty-one years, and twenty-two to twenty-six years. Wages in these categories averaged JD 84.300, JD 71.200, and JD 85.200, respectively. These wage averages were less than the overall average by 19%-33%. The table also shows that wage averages increased considerably in the middle age brackets (twenty-seven to thirty-one, thirty-two to thirty-six, thirty-seven to forty-one, forty-two to forty-six) from JD 103.200, which was close to the overall average, to JD 119.300 and JD 132.600, before dropping again to JD 112.200 in the category fifty-seven to sixty-one. They then rose to JD 118.800 in the older than sixty-one age group. The average wages of Jordanians in the various age groups were higher than the overall averages, while wages for non-Jordanians were lower, although both were in fact close in their distribution and pattern to the overall averages. Wage averages tended to rise with the age and experience of the worker until the age of forty-six, and began to drop thereafter.

Obviously, the data of Table 5.6 would produce an inverted U-shape curve for the age span of seventeen to sixty-one (seventeen to fifty-six for non-Jordanians). The relatively high wage averages for people younger than seventeen and older than sixty-one and the peak level around the age of forty-one need further study. Probably, the peak level is linked to the development process of Jordan's laborpower; the relatively high wages at very low and very high age may be due to the small percentage of people working at this age in combination with their specific incentives and job characteristics.

TABLE 5.6
Monthly Average for Private Sector Workers by Age, 1987 (JD)

Age	Jordanians	Non-Jordanians	Total
Less than 17	85.260	81.920	84.250
17-21	72.200	68.040	71.220
22-26	88.190	77.940	85.200
27-31	113.510	89.990	103.150
32-36	135.770	100.840	119.260
37-41	146.530	111.190	132.610
42-46	139.390	116.520	132.430
47-51	125.120	110.500	121.470
52-56	114.770	107.870	113.390
57-61	111.680	115.310	112.200
62+	121.040	102.100	118.780
Total	109.930	93.680	104.370

Source: Social Security Corporation, computer section.

2.6 Wage Distribution by Marital Status

Table 5.7 shows that the highest wage average was that of married people, reaching JD 118.600 (JD 125.500 for Jordanians and JD 101.800 for non-Jordanians). The wage averages of Jordanians in all other categories were higher than those of non-Jordanians except for widows and widowers. Wage averages for non-Jordanians in this category were higher than any other (JD 148.500). Moreover, the lowest wage averages went to divorcées and divorcés (JD 79.800), where Jordanians' wage averages (JD 79.800) were almost the same as those of non-Jordanians (JD 80.100).

2.7 Wage Distribution by Area of Origin

Table 5.8 shows that the overall wage average of Jordanians, JD 109.900, was higher than that of non-Jordanians, which stood at JD 93.700, producing an overall average of JD 104.400. Multiplying these averages by the number of workers in each category shows that the overall value of wages paid to workers subject to social security regulations was JD 41.59 million monthly, or JD 499 million annually. Of this JD 28.28 million monthly (JD 345.85 million annually) went to Jordanians, while JD 12.8 million monthly (JD 153.20 million annually) went to non-Jordanians.

Despite the fact that wage averages of Jordanians were higher than those of non-Jordanians, closer examination of Table 5.8 shows clearly that wage averages of some groups of non-Jordanians were two or three times higher those of Jordanians. The average wage of Australians was JD 300; of Europeans, JD 273.230; of Americans, JD 259.200; and of non-Arab Asians, JD 119.800. These figures can be explained by the small numbers of workers from these parts of the world: 24 Australians, 2,487 Europeans, and 440 Americans. Moreover, these workers were usually highly qualified personnel who were invited to Jordan to answer specific needs in the absence of adequate local expertise; hence, they usually received very high salaries. Those who earned more than JD 500 included 12.5% of the Australians, 23.4% of the Europeans, and 15.7% of the Americans, com-

TABLE 5.7
Average Monthly Wage by Marital Status, 1987 (JD)

Marital Status	Jordanians	Non-Jordanians	Total
Single	95.870	83.890	91.760
Married	125.530	101.810	118.550
Widowed	94.740	148.450	105.450
Divorced	79.790	80.080	79.810
Total	109.930	93.680	104.370

Source: Social Security Corporation, computer section.

TABLE 5.8
Average Monthly Wage by Worker Place of Origin, 1987 (JD)

Place of Origin	Average Monthly Wage (JD)
Jordan	109.930
Arab countries	80.110
African countries (non-Arab)	90.890
Asian countries (non-Arab)	119.810
Australia	300.000
Europe	273.230
Americas (north and south)	259.200
Total	104.370

Source: Social Security Corporation, computer section.

pared to 0.59% of the Jordanians, 0.87% of the Asians, and 0.41% of the non-Jordanian Arabs covered by the study (see Table 5A.5). In fact, all the Australians received more than JD 100, and none was in the two lower wage brackets.

The lowest wage bands included a high concentration of non-Jordanian Arabs, Africans, Jordanians, and Asians. The group receiving less than JD 150 included 84.6% of the Arabs, 74.8% of the Africans, 62.4% of the Jordanians, and 46.9% of the Asians, compared with only 15.9% of the Americans and 24.6% of the Europeans. The highest wage bands included a high concentration of Europeans, Americans, and Australians. The JD 300+ category included among its number 40.8%, 34.5%, and 33.3% of these groups, respectively, compared with 3.12% of the Jordanians, 3% of the Asians, 2.4% of the Africans, and 0.85% of the non-Jordanian Arabs covered by the study.

3. Summary and Conclusions

The foregoing analysis of the wage averages and distribution categories for private sector workers subject to social security regulations points to the following:

- The overall average wage is JD 104; JD 110 for Jordanians and JD 93.700 for non-Jordanians. Based on this, the total of wages paid to workers who are subject to social security regulations is around JD 500 million annually, of which JD 345 million goes to Jordanians and JD 153 million is paid to non-Jordanians.
- Wage averages of Jordanians are higher than those of non-Jordanians. This is true of wage averages in most sectors and for most pro-

fessional groups, with the exception of two sectors--finance/insurance, and tourism--and two professional categories--manager and technician/specialist.
- These same sectors and professional categories earn the highest wages of all sectors and professional categories.
- The lowest wage averages go to the agricultural, service, and manufacturing sectors.
- The majority of workers who are subject to social security regulations receive low wages (67% receive less than JD 100, and 87% receive less than 150 JD). Those receiving higher wages are few (7% receive more than JD 200, and 4% earn more than JD 300).
- The overall average wage of male workers is higher than that of female workers. The average wage of Jordanian females is lower than that of non-Jordanian females.
- The governorates of Karak and Amman, respectively, offer the two highest wage averages. The lowest wage averages are offered by Balqa and Irbid, respectively. In these two governorates, non-Jordanians receive higher wage averages than do Jordanians.
- Wage averages are low in the lower age groups. Wage averages rise through the age groups and years of experience but drop again in the higher age brackets.
- Married people and non-Jordanian widowers and widows receive the highest wages of their respective categories.
- Although the average wage of Jordanians is higher than that of non-Jordanians, certain groups (Australians, Europeans, and Americans) receive up to two or three times the average wages of Jordanians. The lowest wage averages go to non-Jordanian Arab and African workers.

6

Male-Female Wage Differentiation by Economic Activity and Education

Ahmad Malkawi

1. Introduction

Discussion of the problem of income distribution constitutes an important body of the literature on economics. Examination of the relevant theories reveals that they focus either on equity of income distribution or on marginal productivity of labor.

The measurement of equity highlights income distribution but does not adequately explain the underlying reasons for the inequality of income distribution. The theory of marginal productivity of labor suggests that productivity is the main factor affecting income, so we can understand why the income of a qualified engineer is higher than the income of an unskilled worker.[1] Unfortunately, this theory does not offer a satisfactory explanation for income variation among different groups such as males and females or rural and urban groups, nor does it explain why the incomes of females are low.

The income of females could be low not because of their capability and productivity but because of serious barriers that prevented them from acquiring the necessary skills and education, a lack of equal opportunities, and their lack of entrance into the labor market at the first opportunity.[2] This may account for a specific part of the gap between the income of the two sexes and that of other groupings in society and may of course account for a good part of the male/female income differential, but it cannot account for all differences. Even where equal opportunities do exist, factors causing income differentials will prevail because of physical differences between men and women and because of other circumstances: for example, delayed entry to the labor market or exit from it for reasons relating to pregnancy and childcare or a spouse's employment move.[3]

Fifty years ago, agriculture was the dominant economic activity in Jordan. Women played an important role in farming and animal husbandry in rural areas. In urban areas, the role of women traditionally was restricted to the home. A traditional lifestyle did not facilitate the acquisition of necessary education and skills that a woman needed in order to play an equal role in society. Since the early 1950s, such constraints have been eroding. Opportunities for education have widened and increased.[4] The proportion of females in schools today is almost equal to their proportion in the total population of the same age. Unfortunately, wage differentials between women and men still exist, and this problem has not received sufficient official or government attention. Therefore, this chapter aims to identify and describe this problem in institutions employing five or more persons in the various economic sectors.

1.1 Conjectures

This chapter is based on three assumptions:

1. Despite the fact that Jordanian labor law prohibits discrimination according to sex, race, or religion[5] in practice sex/wage differentials are apparent in most economic sectors, except the public sector.
2. Wage variation decreases as socioeconomic development increases.
3. There will be less wage variation among working groups of the same educational level.

The extent of wage differentials between males and females, the reasons for them, and their persistence have been studied in detail in various countries.[6] But such a study has not been conducted in Jordan thus far.

1.2 Scope and Limitations

The study on which this chapter is based covered institutions employing five persons or more during the period 1980-1986 and relied on data from an employment survey published by the Department of Statistics, which excluded all personnel of Jordan Armed Forces and Public Security. (There was a lack of available data from other sources.) Thus, the study covered one-third of the labor force in Jordan. The total number of employees in the economic sectors covered by the study increased from 118,000 in 1980 to 174,000 in 1986.

The percentage of females included in that number increased from 20.8% in 1980 to 22.9% in 1986. The percentage of females in the various economic sectors ranged from 1% to 30%. During the period of this study, Jordan became a labor-importing country. According to the employment survey, the percentage of foreign nationals constituted 8% of the total number of employees; of these 9% were females.

The period covered by the study can be divided into two phases. The first phase, 1980-1982, was characterized by an economic boom, and the second phase, 1983-1986, was characterized by economic stagnation.

The chapter will attempt to analyze the following topics for the whole period:

1. Evolution of wage differentials among all workers by economic activity in all establishments with five or more employees.
2. Wage differentials among all workers according to economic activity and size of establishment.
3. Wage differentials among graduates according to economic activity in all establishments with 5 or more employees.
4. Wage differentials among graduates according to economic activity and size of establishment.
5. Comparison of differentials between graduates and all employees in all establishments according to economic activity and size of establishment.

1.3 Methodology and Statistical Analysis

The following methods of analysis were used in the study:

- Wages of females were calculated as a percentage of the male's wage, which was assumed to be 100%. Wage differentials were examined in terms of this percentage in each sector for the period 1980-1986 and for all employees and for graduates as a separate group.[7]
- For the year 1986 only, wages of females were calculated as a percentage of the male's wage for all employees and for graduates according to the size of establishment and economic sector.
- The geometric average wage was calculated for wage variation of females by the formula [8]:

$$GA = \sqrt[n]{W_1 \times W_2 \times ... \times W_n} \qquad (1)$$

where: GA = geometric average of wage variation
W_i = the variation of female's wage in year i
n = number of years

- Finally, the standard deviation for males and females wages was calculated by economic sector as follows [9]:

$$SD = \sqrt{\frac{1}{n-1} \Sigma \, (W - \overline{W})^2} \qquad (2)$$

where: SD = standard deviation
         W = wage rate
         $\overline{W}$ = average wage for all sectors
         n = number of sectors.

2. Findings

2.1 Participation of Women in the Labor Market

The participation of women in economic activity developed slowly during the period under consideration. Table 6A.1 in the Appendix indicates that the percentage of working females in the various economic activities increased from 20.8% in 1980 to 22.9% of the total work force for these sectors by 1986. The percentage increase was very low and amounted to only 1.6% each year. On average, the proportion of women in the work force during the whole period was 21% for all employees irrespective of their level of education.

The participation of women graduates in economic activity in establishments with five employees or more increased greatly during the period under consideration. The proportion of graduate women among all graduate employees increased from 16.4% in 1980 to 24.1% in 1986, an average annual increase of 6.7%; this was much higher than the percentage increase for all employees as shown in Table 6A.2.

2.2 Wage Differentials for all Employees

Table 6.1 shows that there were differentials between the wages of males and females in almost all areas of economic activity between 1980 and 1986 in establishments with five or more employees. The biggest recorded difference between the wages of males and females was in the manufacturing sector. This difference could be explained in part by the fact that certain tasks in the manufacturing sector are traditionally carried out by women and do not require much physical effort; thus the pay is low.

The smallest difference in wages was found in three different sectors at various stages in the period under study: transport and storage, construction, and commerce. In the transport sector, the differentials were in favor of females over males for the years 1980, 1981, 1984, and 1985. This difference can be mainly attributed to the Royal Jordanian Airlines, which employs many females, a high proportion of whom are foreigners paid relatively high salaries. Similarly, in the construction sector, differentials

TABLE 6.1
Females' Wages as a Percentage of Males' Wages, 1980-1986

Sector [a]	1980	1981	1982	1983	1984	1985	1986	Average
Mining and quarrying	0.82	0.70	0.79	0.73	0.82	0.71	0.76	0.76
Manufacturing	0.59	0.64	0.60	0.63	0.58	0.57	0.63	0.60
Electricity, gas, and water	0.75	0.73	0.82	0.83	0.91	0.79	0.82	0.81
Construction	0.88	0.93	1.20	1.23	1.00	0.92	0.88	1.00
Commerce	0.90	1.01	0.98	0.97	0.93	1.02	0.96	0.97
Transport and storage	1.10	1.10	0.69	0.98	1.46	1.02	0.83	1.00
Financial services	0.65	0.66	0.71	0.72	0.68	0.67	0.66	0.68
Community services and public administration	0.90	0.90	0.87	0.90	0.87	0.86	0.87	0.88

[a] For establishments with five or more employees.

Source: Department of Statistics, *Employment Survey* (various issues).

were in favor of females in 1982 and 1983. For all other activities, males' wages were higher than females' wages for the period.

The greatest geometric average variation over the whole period occurred in the manufacturing sector, whereas the smallest geometric average variation occurred in the commercial sector. This standard also showed that the construction and transport sectors revealed no wage variation, on average, for the period.

2.3 Wage Differentials for University Graduates

As shown in Table 6.2, the highest wage differentials in establishments with five or more employees were found in the construction sector and in mining and quarrying. For 1981 and 1984, differentials were higher in construction than in mining and quarrying; for the years 1980, 1982, 1983, 1985, and 1986, the situation was reversed.

For the entire period, no general trend for wage differentials was recorded. Some economic sectors showed decreasing differentials as wages of females increased throughout the period. Other economic sectors showed increasing differentials. These sectors included public administration, financial services, and electricity and water.

Tables 6.1 and 6.2 show that, in general, wage differentials were higher for university graduates than for all employees.

2.4 Wage Differentials for all Employees and for University Graduates

Table 6.3 shows the following:

TABLE 6.2
Female Graduates' Wages as a Percentage of Male Graduates' Wages, 1980-1986

Sector [a]	1980	1981	1982	1983	1984	1985	1986	Average
Mining and quarrying	0.41	0.47	0.50	0.49	0.60	0.46	0.53	0.49
Manufacturing	0.57	0.62	0.62	0.79	0.61	0.63	0.68	0.64
Electricity, gas, and water	0.51	0.68	0.96	0.55	0.60	0.53	0.54	0.61
Construction	0.45	0.63	0.63	0.62	0.51	0.49	0.59	0.51
Commerce	0.56	0.67	0.62	0.59	0.68	0.66	0.72	0.64
Transport and storage	0.69	0.81	0.53	0.72	0.71	0.70	0.65	0.68
Financial services	0.56	0.55	0.56	0.55	0.54	0.56	0.55	0.55
Community services and public administration	0.74	0.75	0.75	0.76	0.75	0.72	0.69	0.74

[a] For establishments with five ore more employees.

Source: Department of Statistics, *Employment Survey* (various issues).

1. For establishments with five or more employees, the manufacturing sector showed the biggest wage variation for all employees, while the biggest variation for university graduates occurred in the mining and quarrying sector.
2. For establishments with five to nine employees, financial services revealed the biggest wage variation for all employees, while for university graduates, the manufacturing sector revealed the biggest variation.
3. For establishments with ten to twenty-four employees, the manufacturing sector showed the greatest wage variation for all employees, whereas financial services showed the greatest variation for university graduates.
4. For establishments with twenty-five or more employees, again, the manufacturing sector revealed the greatest variation for all employees, while the construction sector recorded the greatest variation for graduates.
5. The smallest wage differentials were found in the commercial sector for all employees in all establishments. Moreover, the wages of females were higher than males' wages in establishments with five to nine and ten to twenty-four employees. This sector was also characterized by the smallest wage differentials for university graduates in all establishments with fewer than twenty-five employees.
6. The highest geometric average variation during the entire period occurred in the mining and quarrying sector, while the smallest one occurred in the community services and public administration sectors.

TABLE 6.3
Females' Wages as a Percentage of Males' Wages by Size of Establishment and Major Activities, 1986

Economic Activity	All Establishments		5-9 Employees		10-24 Employees		25 or more Employees	
	E	G	E	G	E	G	E	G
Mining and quarrying	0.76	0.53	-a	-	-	-	0.74	0.53
Manufacturing	0.63	0.68	0.77	0.48	0.53	-	0.61	0.68
Electricity, gas and water	0.82	0.54	-	-	-	-	0.82	0.54
Construction	0.88	0.59	0.70	0.60	0.89	0.94	0.83	0.50
Commerce	0.96	0.72	1.07	0.81	1.11	0.94	0.89	0.60
Transport and storage	0.83	0.65	0.80	0.57	0.90	0.54	0.82	0.68
Financial services	0.66	0.55	0.68	0.55	0.53	0.47	0.66	0.55
Community, services and public administration	0.87	0.69	0.74	0.64	0.86	0.77	0.87	0.69
Total	0.78	0.61	0.81	0.60	0.72	0.65	0.77	0.67

E = All Employees
G = Graduates
a   Means no females were found to compare them with male wages.

Source: Department of Statistics, *Employment Survey* (various issues).

2.5 Standard Deviation of Wages for All Sectors

Table 6.4 shows the calculated standard deviations of wages both for all employees and for university graduates in all sectors. For all employees, the standard deviation of females' wages was higher than that of males for the period 1980-1984, but the situation was reversed for 1985-1986. For university graduates, the standard deviation of females' wages was lower than that of males throughout the entire period.

TABLE 6.4
Standard Deviation of Wages for all Sectors

Workers	1980		1981		1982		1983		1984		1985		1986	
	M	F	M	F	M	F	M	F	M	F	M	F	M	F
All workers	23.2	24.1	27.3	30.9	30.3	39.3	32.6	36.2	40.0	54.1	38.0	33.0	41.1	30.7
University graduates	81.7	22.3	65.1	23.2	99.4	52.0	84.8	48.5	87.8	36.1	79.5	31.2	83.2	43.1

Source: Calculated from Tables 6A.3 and 6A.4.

3. Conclusions

3.1 Results of the Statistical Analysis

1. Throughout the period under consideration, the participation of males in economic activity was on average four times higher than that of females. The participation of female university graduates in the labor market was growing faster than that of nongraduate females. This bore witness to the increasing participation of women in university education, which expanded in the 1970s and the 1980s. Furthermore, the majority of females enrolled in arts faculties, where most courses of study could be completed in a year or two less than it took for a science cource. Additionally, females were not delayed in their entry to the labor market by the two years of military service compulsory for males.

2. Males' wages were higher than females' wages both for all workers and for university graduates taken as a separate group.

3. For all employees, the most highly paid females were found in the transport, construction, and commercial sectors.

4. For university graduates, the highest females' wages were found in the community service, public administration, transport, and commercial sectors.

5. In general, the geometric average for wage variations of females was lower for university graduates than for all employees.

6. The standard deviation of wages was greater for males than for females in all sectors for the entire period.

7. On average, the wage differentials of females were higher for university graduates than for all employees because many males were educated at university before the boom in university education for women. Hence, there was a group of graduate males with seniority over their female graduate colleagues.

8. The wage differentials between males and females in Jordan could be explained in part by the following:

- Because of rising cost, some establishments dismissed females when they married, thereby making it impossible for them to acquire seniority.
- During periods of economic recession, there was a general tendency to hire more females because they were willing to accept lower wages than males were.
- Females tended to prefer to work locally even if they got lower wages than they would elsewhere, because they could then more easily balance their work with their domestic duties.

- Females, in general, were not able to do evening work, which deprived them of overtime. Some establishments adopted a system whereby the full working day was split into two periods with a break in the middle. This did not suit many females, who as a result either had to resign or work only the first half of the day and accept a correspondingly low wage.

3.2 Answers to the Conjectures

The results of the study suggest that (1) sex/wage differentials are greater for university graduates than for all employees;(2) sex wage differentials do not get narrower with economic growth through the years; and (3) for 1986, sex/wage differentials were greater for university graduates than for all employees whatever the size of the establishment.

Notes

1. Robert, B. et al: *A History of Economic Theory and Methods* (New York: McGraw-Hill, 1975), pp. 381-383.
2. Sloane, P.J.: "The Structure of Labour Market and Low Pay for Women," in Sloane, P.J. (ed.): *Women and Low Pay* (London: Macmillan, 1980).
3. Chiplin, B., and Sloane, P.J.: "Male/Female Earnings Differences: A Further Analysis," *British Journal of Industrial Relations* (1976).
4. For further discussion see: Mazen Odeh: "Some Effects That Accompanied Woman's Work in Jordan." (Ministry of Labor and Social Development) *Labor Magazine*, nos. 25-26 (1984)/(Arabic).
5. Jordan has approved international agreement no. 100 on the man-woman wage equalization in equal work. See: *Labor Magazine*, nos. 27-28 (1984).
6. See: Turner, H.A.: "Inflation and Wage Differentials in Great Britain," in Dunlop, J.T. (ed.): *The Theory of Wage Discrimination* (London: Macmillan, 1955); Ben-Yosef, T.: "Analysis of Earnings Differentials Between Men and Women in Israel," Paper no. 7610 (Jerusalem: Falle Institute, 1971).
7. Fanny, Ginor: *Socio-Economic Disparities in Israel* (Tel Aviv: University Publishing Projects, 1979), p. 103.
8. Donald, S. et al: *Statistics: A Fresh Approach* (New York: McGraw-Hill, 1980), p. 60.
9. MacEachron, A.E.: *Basic Statistics in the Human Service* (Baltimore, Md.: University Park Press, 1982), p. 88.

Bibliography

Ben-Yosef, T.: "Analysis of Earnings Differntials Between Men and Women in Israel." Paper no. 7610. Jerusalem: Falle Institute, 1971.
Chiplin, B., and Sloane, P.J.: "Male/Female Earnings Differences: A Further Analysis." *British Journal of Industrial Relations* (1976).

Donald, S. et al: Statistics: *A Fresh Approach*. New York: McGraw-Hill, 1980.

Fanny, Ginor: *Socio-Economic Disparities in Israel*. Tel Aviv: University Publishing Projects, 1979.

MacEachron, A.E.: *Basic Statistics in the Human Service*. Baltimore, Md.: University Park Press, 1982.

Odeh, M.: "Some Effects That Accompanied Woman's Work in Jordan." *Labor Magazine*, nos. 25-26 (1984)/(Arabic).

Robert, B. et al: *A History of Economic Theory and Methods*. New York: McGraw-Hill, 1975.

Sloane, P.J.: "The Structure of Labour Market and Low Pay for Women." In Sloane, P.J. (ed.): *Women and Low Pay*. London: Macmillan, 1980.

Turner, H.A.: "Inflation and Wage Differentials in Great Britain." In Dunlop, J.T. (ed.): *The Theory of Wage Discrimination*. London: Macmillan, 1955.

7

Income Distribution and Its Social Impact in the Occupied Territories

Abdelfattah Abu Shokor

1. Introduction

The theory of the distribution of income can be divided into two major fields. The first is called the functional distribution of income and the second the personal distribution of income. The first is concerned with defining the shares of the different production factors of the national income. In other words, this field defines the wage rates, salaries, and rates of profit. The second field deals with the study of the distribution of income among individuals or families, the differentials in distribution among them, and the reasons behind these differentials.

In this chapter, the distribution of personal income in the Occupied Territories--the West Bank and Gaza Strip--and the social impact of this distribution will be examined. Therefore, the chapter will try to answer the following questions:

- What is the pattern of income distribution in the Occupied Territories?
- What inequalities are there in the distribution of income among individuals or families, and what is the degree of concentration of that income?
- What is the nature of income distribution among the different regions (governorates or major areas)?
- What are the reasons for inequalities in income distribution?
- What is the impact of income distribution on family size? On standard of living? On class structure?

This chapter is based on a study completed in December 1987 under the title "The Social Class Structure and the Pattern of Income Distribution in the West Bank and Gaza Strip." This study, which was done at request of An-Najah University in Nablus, was classified but unpublished; data used in it were collected through a field survey carried out in the summer of 1985.

The sample size used in the study was 1,182. This sample represented families in both the West Bank and Gaza Strip. The stratified random sample was chosen by dividing the population into three principal strata--cities, villages, and refugee camps. In the rural areas some of the villages were too small to be efficient primary sampling units (PSU). These were amalgamated with neighboring ones to form reasonably efficient PSUs. This random sample was made self-weighting with an expected sampling fraction of 0.5% and a precision of ±3%.

2. The Pattern of Income Distribution in the Occupied Territories

In order to deal with the way income is distributed in the Occupied Territories, we have to define the meaning of income and income groups. Income means the personal income available for the benefit of the family or the cash income a person earns from all sources--that is, from work done in the West Bank, Gaza Strip, or the Israeli labor market or from the ownership of properties or shares in the agricultural, industrial, construction, trade, transportation, or other sectors. Income also includes remittances from family members or relatives abroad, retirement pensions, and any money received from social institutions or *zakah* (alms tax). Income as defined here is net income; it does not include those public services that the family gets free of charge, such as health care and education.

Income groups are composed of families. No distinction was made according to whether families depended on one person or on more than one. Families were classified according to income as follows: top income group, with an income of JD 601 and more per month; upper income group, with an income of JD 401-600 per month; middle income group, with an income of JD 201-400 per month; low income group, with an income of JD 101-200 per month; bottom income group, with an income of JD 100 or less per month.

Table 7A.1 shows the distribution of families in the West Bank and Gaza Strip based on the preceding income classification. It can be seen that 2.73% of the families in the West Bank were in the top income group. Most members of this group (85%) were concentrated in the cities. The rest were distributed between the refugee camps and rural areas, with 10% and 5%, respectively.

The top income group in the Gaza Strip was represented by only 1.1%

of the total number of families; 60% of these well-off families lived in cities and 40% lived in rural areas. This group included the big landowners who could afford to use modern machinery and methods of agriculture and thereby take advantage of the ready availability of water. (Shortage of water has the effect of limiting the number of big landlords, except in the few areas where water is readily available, such as in the Jordan Valley and the northern parts of the West Bank.)

The upper income group was larger than the top income group both in the West Bank and the Gaza Strip; it accounts for 4.91% of families in the former area and 3.53% in the latter. But as far as the geographic distribution was concerned, in the West Bank this income group was largely concentrated in the cities (66.6%), whereas in the Gaza Strip, 55.2% of these families lived in urban areas, 25% in camps, and 18.7% in rural areas.

The middle income group, which along with the upper income group constituted the middle class, was not large, including as it did about 21.72% of the families in the West Bank and 13.49% of those in the Gaza Strip. That the group was smaller in Gaza indicated, as shall be seen later, that there was a large group of people living below the poverty line in Gaza.

In the West Bank the middle income group was concentrated in the cities and villages, where 57.8% and 22.9% of the total resided, respectively. In the Gaza Strip 49.1% of this group was found in the cities and

TABLE 7.1

Distribution of Families in West Bank and Gaza Strip According to Area and Level of Income, 1985

Area	Top Income		Upper Income		Middle Income		Low Income		Bottom Income	
	No.	%	No	%	No.	%	No.	%	No.	%
Jenin	3	15.00	2	5.56	29	18.24	40	20.10	33	10.38
Nablus	7	35.00	12	33.33	27	16.98	34	17.09	44	13.84
Toulkarm	5	25.00	8	22.22	35	22.01	36	18.09	37	11.64
Hebron	1	5.00	6	16.67	21	13.21	37	18.59	78	24.53
Ramallah, Jerusalem and Jericho	4	20.00	6	16.67	39	24.53	49	24.62	109	34.28
Bethlehem	-	-	2	5.56	8	5.03	3	1.51	17	5.34
Total	20	100.00	36	100.00	159	100.00	199	100.00	318	100.00

Source: Abu Shokor, A.F.: "Social Structure and Pattern of Income Distribution in the West Bank and Gaza Strip,"Nablus: An-Najah National University, January 1987, unpublished.

37.7% in the camps.

The low income group and the bottom income group (families living below the poverty line) made up the poor in society. According to Table 7A.1, 27.2% of the West Bank families and 24.55% of Gaza Strip families fell into the low income group. In the West Bank, families in this group were distributed as follows: 48.7% in villages, 40.2% in cities, and 11% in camps. In the Gaza Strip they were distributed as follows: 46.85% in camps, 41.44% in cities, and 11.71 % in villages.

The bottom income group was relatively larger in the Gaza Strip (57.3% of the families surveyed) than in the West Bank (43.44%). In the Gaza Strip, 51.74% of these bottom income families lived in the cities and 37.1% lived in the camps. In the West Bank, 36.79% lived in villages, 32.4% lived in camps, and 30.82% lived in the cities.

There was a wide disparity of incomes in the West Bank and the Gaza Strip. There was a large group of poor people. The middle class group was small and the top income group even smaller. The poor were concentrated in the villages, camps, and poor quarters of the cities. The middle, upper, and top income groups were concentrated in the cities.

3. Distribution of Income in the West Bank

In order to clarify the pattern of income distribution in the West Bank, distribution was analyzed according to the six major areas of the official administrative organization: Jenin; Nablus; Toulkarm; Hebron; Ramallah, Jerusalem, and Jericho; and Bethlehem. Table 7.1 shows the distribution of each income group in these areas. The data indicate that top income families were concentrated mainly in northern areas of the West Bank--that is, in Nablus, Toulkarm, and Jenin, where 75% of the high income group was found. The remainder of these well-off families were in Ramallah, Jerusalem, and Jericho (20%) and in Hebron (5%).

The upper income group was also concentrated in Jenin, Nablus, and Toulkarm (61.11%). The rest of the families in this group were found in Ramallah, Jerusalem, and Jericho (16.67%); Hebron (16.67%); and Bethlehem (5.56%).

The middle income group was concentrated mainly in Ramallah, Jerusalem, and Jericho (24.53%) and in Toulkarm (22.01%). This was followed by Jenin, with 18.24% of the families in this group; Nablus, with 16.98%; Hebron, with 13.21%; and Bethlehem, with 5.03%.

The families in the low income group were distributed fairly evenly among the different areas. Ramallah, Jerusalem, and Jericho, however, had the highest concentration (24.62%), followed by Jenin (20.1%), Hebron (18.59%), Toulkarm (18.09%), and Nablus (17.09%).

The concentration of the first three income groups in the northern areas of the West Bank indicated that poorer groups were concentrated in the central and southern regions. The data in Table 7.1 indicate that 64.15% of these poorer families were concentrated in Ramallah, Jerusalem, and Jericho; Hebron; and Bethlehem.

4. Ratio of Income Concentration

An awareness of the distribution of family income across the different income groups is insufficient to give a complete picture of the inequality in income distribution and the reasons for the inequality. The ratio of income concentration must be measured because this will show in whose hands the income is concentrated and will allow us to compare the inequality of income distribution in the West Bank and Gaza Strip with the situation in other developing countries. In order to show the inequality of income distribution in the West Bank, the Lorenz curve was used, and the ratio of income concentration was calculated by means of the Gini concentration ratio.

Table 7.2 shows the inequality of income distribution in the West Bank and Gaza Strip, the cumulative percentages of families, and the real income they earned. From these data Lorenz curves for the West Bank and Gaza Strip, both separately and together, were drawn (see Figures 7A.1, 7A.2, and 7.1). It should be noted here that in each figure the difference between the Lorenz curve and the 45° line represents the inequality of income distribution: in the West Bank and Gaza Strip separately (Figures 7A.1 and 7A.2); and in the West Bank and Gaza Strip together (Figure 7.1). By looking at the figures, we can see that the variation and

TABLE 7.2
Percentage Distribution of Families in the West Bank and Gaza Strip by Cumulative Level of Income, 1985

West Bank		Gaza Strip		West Bank and Gaza Strip	
% Families	% Income	% Families	% Income	% Families	% Income
43.44	18.30	57.30	29.70	48.73	21.98
70.62	40.94	81.85	56.47	74.91	45.95
92.34	74.52	95.34	81.85	93.49	76.89
97.25	87.75	98.87	94.02	97.88	89.78
99.98	99.98	99.79	99.96	99.98	99.98
100.00	100.00	100.00	100.00	100.00	100.00

Source: Abu Shokor, A.F.: "Social Structure and Pattern of Income Distribution in the West Bank and Gaza Strip," Nablus: An-Najah National University, January 1987, unpublished.

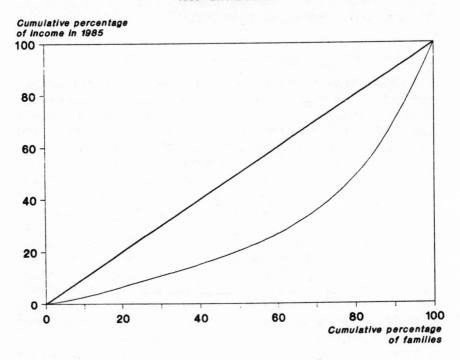

FIGURE 7.1
Variation in Income Distribution in the West Bank and Gaza Strip,
1985– Lorenz Curve

inequality in income distribution in the West Bank is less marked than it is in the Gaza Strip. This becomes clearer if the ratio of income distribution in each area is measured by means of the Gini concentration ratio.

The ratio of income concentration or variation in income distribution reached 0.4580 in the West Bank and Gaza Strip taken together, the figures for the areas taken separately being 0.4230 for the West Bank and 0.4450 [1] for the Gaza Strip. If we compare this with the situation in other developing countries, we find that the ratio of income concentration in the West Bank and Gaza was close to the ratio found in the Asiatic countries, where it reached a concentration of income of 0.4369,[2] but it was less than that found in countries of Africa and Latin America, where the concentration of income reached 0.5128 and 0.5134, respectively.[3] The degree of income concentration in the West Bank and Gaza Strip was greater than in Israel, where it stood at 0.3128.[4]

5. Reasons for Inequality of Income Distribution

From this analysis, it can be seen that the distribution of income in the West Bank and Gaza Strip was characterized by inequality and resembled the pattern of income distribution in the developing countries of Asia. We must examine the reasons for this variation and inequality because awareness of the reasons for inequality must form the basis of any economic policy aimed at improving the standard of living of all families in the West Bank and Gaza Strip.

The rise in unemployment or the lack of job vacancies is considered to be one of the major reasons behind the inequality of income distribution in the West Bank and Gaza Strip. The data in Table 7A.2 show that the unemployment rate in its simple definition [5] reached 10.02% in both the West Bank and Gaza Strip. It is also obvious that the poorer classes were the most seriously affected by unemployment, which was concentrated mainly among families below the poverty line (not more than JD 100 income per month) and families with low incomes. We find that 57.62% of the unemployed were from families below poverty line, and 22.86% were from low income families. The unemployed from the middle class made up 13.55% of the total unemployed. The percentage of unemployed in the top two income groups was only 3.38 and 2.54, respectively.

By looking at the rate and distribution of unemployment among the different income groups in the West Bank and Gaza Strip taken separately, we find that unemployment in the West Bank at 10.85% was higher than unemployment in the Gaza Strip, which was 8.68%. Unemployment in the Gaza Strip was widespread among the two poorest groups, which accounted for 89.73% of the total number of unemployed. In the West Bank, these groups accounted for 75.93% of the total.

There was no unemployment in the top income group in the Gaza Strip, but the unemployment rate was 3.79% in this group in the West Bank. There was also very little unemployment in the second group in the Gaza Strip (5.12%), the rate being even lower than this (2.53%) in the West Bank. Unemployment in the middle income group in the West Bank (17.72%) was higher than it was in the Gaza Strip (5.12%).

Concerning the spread of unemployment or lack of employment opportunities in the West Bank and Gaza Strip, we find that the variation of ownership among the families and the income generated were two factors that led to the inequality of income distribution. Other factors were extra work done in the Israeli labor market [6] and internal and external money transfers.

Data on sources of additional income are contained in Table 7A.3. According to these data, 19.85% of families in the West Bank and Gaza Strip had an additional income from agriculture, 17.4% from industry, 18.16% from construction, 20.78% from trade, 6.93% from transportation, 16.05% from rents of houses or land, 23.06% from public or private services, 9.80% from extra work in the Israeli labor market, 3.97% from outside money transfers from relatives abroad, 1.52% from retirement, 1.1% from social welfare, 1.35% from *zakah*, 0.17% from national insurance, and 0.17% from old age funds. There was no difference in sources of additional income between the families in the West Bank or Gaza Strip.

If we compare additional sources of income for each income group in the West Bank and Gaza Strip, we see first that additional income from the different sources came mainly to families in the top income group, the upper income group, and the middle income group. Only a small percentage of families in the low income group and the group below the poverty line received some additional income from the previously mentioned sources. The top income families in the Gaza Strip got their additional income mainly from agriculture (60% of families), trade (40%), rents of houses and real estate (40%), and work in public and private services (20%). As for the top income families in the West Bank, the additional income came from farming (30% of the families), industry (10%), construction (10%), trade (40%), rents of houses or real estate (35%), public or private services (25%), and the Israeli labor market (15%). Most of latter was contracting work.

One of the major reasons for the variation or inequality in income in the West Bank and Gaza Strip was the concentration of the heads of the families in the group below the poverty line and the low income group in subsistence economic sectors that suffered from instability. From Table 7A.4 we find that 19.41% of the group below the poverty line worked in construction, which was characterized by wide seasonal variation and instability. In addition, most of them were unskilled laborers.[7] We also find that 16.64% of the same group worked in industry or handicrafts that were not very well developed, such as carpentry, tailoring, mechanics, and shoemaking.[8] The Table also shows that 23.75% of the group worked in the service sector (private and public) as, for example, messengers, guards, teachers, or imams.[9] We also find that 15.25% of the same group worked in trade as owners of small shops and grocery stores.[10] Another 8.84% worked in agriculture as agricultural workers or small farm owners.[11] Of the rest, 3.81% worked in the transportation sector. The distribtuion in the low income group was not much different: 16.77% worked in industry and handicrafts, 33.5% in the public and private services, 15.48% in trade (owners of grocery stores and small shops), 11.91% in construction, 7.42% in agriculture, and 5.81% in transportation.

The situation did not differ for the West Bank and Gaza Strip either separately or jointly.

6. Social Implications of Income Distribution

6.1 Average Family Size

Average family size in the West Bank and Gaza Strip was big for all income groups. The average family size in both areas was higher than in the East Bank of Jordan. Table 7.3 shows that the average family size was 7.38 persons, while it was 6.4 in the East Bank of Jordan in 1979.[12] For comparative purposes the average family size in Israel in 1986 was 3.84.[13] The large family size for the different income groups in the West Bank and Gaza Strip indicated a high dependency ratio in every group, especially the low income group and the group below the poverty line.

If we compare average family size in the West Bank with that in the Gaza Strip, we find that the latter was larger: 8.1 persons compared to 6.99. This applied to each income group across the board.

In the Gaza Strip, the average family size in the low income group was larger (8.63) than in the other groups. This was followed by the middle income group (8.42), the top income group, and the upper income group (8 persons each). The average family size for the group below the poverty line was the lowest (7.85).

Table 7.3 also shows that in the West Bank the largest average family size was in the low income group (7.14), followed by the group below the poverty line, and the middle group, with 6.96 and 6.9, respectively. The average family size was the smallest (6.85) in the upper income groups.

From the previous data we can conclude that distribution of income is independent of family size. Noneconomic factors seem to play an effective

TABLE 7.3

Average Family Size of Different Income Groups in the West Bank and Gaza Strip, 1985

Area	Bottom Income	Low Income	Middle Income	Upper Income	Top Income	Total Income
West Bank	6.96	7.14	6.9	6.85	7.20	6.99
Gaza Strip	7.85	8.63	8.42	8.00	8.00	8.10
West Bank and Gaza Strip	7.39	7.49	7.26	7.22	7.27	7.38

Source: Abu Shokor, A.F.: "Social Structure and Pattern of Income Distribution in the West Bank and Gaza Strip," Nablus: An-Najah National University, January 1987, unpublished.

role in deciding family size.

6.2 Standard of Living Among Income Groups

The standard of living of any group is indicated by the availability of household appliances such as refrigerators, gas cookers, cars, television sets, and so on. The ownership of these goods is a function of social status as well as income. All such items owned by the low income group and the one below the poverty line are secondhand and are frequently brought by merchants of household goods from the Israeli market, where they are usually sold at auction.

The results of this research [14] showed that the overwhelming majority of families in the top two income groups owned a refrigerator, a washing machine, a color T.V., a gas cooker, an electric stove, a solar heating system, a radio, an electric iron, and an electric as well as a kerosene heater. The majority also owned a car. Video recorders and electric water heaters were less widespread. Few families in these groups owned black and white television sets because they were not high social status items.

Although quite a few families in the middle income group did own a refrigerator, a washing machine, a color T.V. and a black and white one, an electric stove, a solar heating system, a radio, an electric iron, and a kerosene and an electric heater, the percentages were smaller than in the previous two groups. A small percentage of the middle income group owned a video or an electric water heater. Only 41.36% owned a car, this percentage being smaller than for the upper two income groups.

The low income group and the group of families below the poverty line owned very few of the household appliances, and most were second-hand. Most families, however, did own a refrigerator, a washing machine, a regular television set, a gas range, a solar heating system, a radio, and an electric iron, but not a color television set or an electric stove, a video recorder, an electric heater, a kerosene heater, or an electric water heater. The results of the research also showed that a very small percentage owned a car. Thus, standard of living of these families was low, as was their income.

6.3 Social Class Structure

Four major social classes make up Palestinian society in the occupied West Bank and Gaza Strip: the upper class, the petite bourgeoisie, the farmers and fellaheen, and the working class.

6.3.1 The Upper Class

The top income group represents the rich upper class of Palestinian society in the West Bank and Gaza Strip. This class is characterized by a small base, and at the time of the study accounted for only 2.11% of the families there: 2.73% of families in the West Bank and 1.1% of families in the Gaza Strip.

This class is made up of the big landowners, the big merchants, and the owners of big manufacturing companies. This class has been subjected to some change in size under occupation. The availability of water in the Gaza Strip, the Jordan Valley, and the northern areas of the West Bank has led to the development of a class of big landowning farmers. Nevertheless, the size of this group has remained small because of Israeli control over the water supply and the confiscation of lands. This policy has prevented the expansion of the base of big landowners and has posed a continual threat of economic ruin.[15]

In contrast to the group of big landowners, the merchant group has prospered under the Israeli occupation because of the wider markets, both the Israeli market and Arab. Nevertheless, the Israeli occupation and the unstable political situation have led many to invest their accumulated financial capital outside the West Bank and Gaza Strip. This explains its very small contribution to the industrialization process.

Israeli control over the markets in the West Bank and Gaza Strip and the flooding of these markets with Israeli goods have led to competition with Arab industry and have thus weakened the appearance and development of an industrial bourgeoisie. Many of the industrial establishments in the West Bank and Gaza Strip have been destroyed by Israeli competition.[16] Hence, the role of the industrial bourgeoisie class in initiating change, developing the economy of the West Bank and Gaza Strip, or transforming the economy into a developed industrial economy is negligible if not nonexistent under present circumstances.

6.3.2 The Petite Bourgeoisie

This class is the middle class in Palestinian society and includes the families from the upper and middle income groups. At the time of the study, this class accounted for 22.97% of the families in the West Bank and Gaza Strip. This class is composed of three major groups.[17] The first group is formed of those who do not own the means of production but who do enjoy a high income, such as academics, engineers, senior teachers, and managers, especially those employed by the United Nations Relief and Works Agency. The second group consists of the self-employed in the service and trade sectors. The size of this group has grown in the West Bank because of the increase in the volume of trade with Israel and the prosperity of the tourist sector. In the Gaza Strip, the size of this group has not increased, although trade with Israel, the West Bank, and the Arab markets (through Jordan) has become a substitute for the Egyptian market lost due to the Israeli occupation.[18]

The third group is made up of owners of small factories and workshops that are family businesses. This group has been seriously affected by Israeli competition, which has led to the destruction of many of these factories and has forced their owners into the ranks of the unemployed, and thereafter into the Israeli market.[19]

6.3.3 The Farmers and Fellaheen

The third social class--the farmers and "fallaheen"--rents land or owns small farms. In economic terms they belong to the low income group and the group of families below the poverty line. Their agricultural production is weak, and there is no surplus most of the time.[20] Therefore, their participation in the market is very limited. The rise in the cost of living coupled which the occupation polices of control over the water supply and the confiscation of land has forced many in this class to leave their land and work in the Israeli economy.[21] As a result, agricultural production has become an additional, rather than a primary, source of income.

6.3.4 The Working Class

Most of the members of the fourth social class, the working class, are in the low income group and the group of families below the poverty line. (Skilled workers are the exception.) The size of this group has increased greatly under Israeli occupation in the West Bank and Gaza Strip due to increased job opportunities. For example, in the period 1970-1986 the number of waged workers in the West Bank increased from 56,500 to 99,800, an increase of 76.64%.[22] In the Gaza Strip alone during the same period the number increased from 35,200 to 64,300, an increase of 82.67%.[23] There are several reasons for this increase in numbers, the most important being the entry of young people into the labor market [24] and the fact that many farmers and shop owners who faced economic ruin as a result of Israeli economic policies[25] joined the workforce.

7. Summary and Conclusions

From the preceding discussion we see that the top income group in Palestinian society is characterized by a small base. The same can be said about the next two groups. At the same time, we see the wide base of the low income group and the group of families below the poverty line, which account for 75% of the total number of families in the West Bank and Gaza Strip. This variation points to widespread poverty and inequality in income distribution. The variation or inequality in income distribution resembles to a great extent the situation in many underdeveloped Asian countries, where inequality is less marked than it is in African and Latin American countries.

The main reasons for the variation or inequality in income distribution in the West Bank and Gaza Strip is the spread of unemployment or lack of job opportunities, the variation in ownership, and the concentration of heads of households in the bottom two groups in those economic sectors that are characterized by underdevelopment and low productivity.

The pattern of income distribution in the West Bank and Gaza Strip has no effect on family size, which is higher on average than in the East Bank and double the average in Israel. Nevertheless, the high family size is reflected in the comparatively low standard of living for most of the families there.

The social class structure of the different income groups is reflected in the formulation of four social classes: the upper class, the petite bourgeoisie, the farmers and the fellaheen, and the working class. Each one of these classes has been subject to continuous changes under the Israeli occupation. [26]

From all of this we can say that raising the standard of living of the lower income groups, especially the middle income group and the group of families below the poverty line, cannot be realized by a policy of redistribution of income. Instead, higher economic growth rates must be achieved, and structural changes in the economy of the West Bank and Gaza Strip must be made to transform it from a deficit economy into a well-developed industrial and agricultural economy.

Notes

1. The value of the Gini concentration ratio is between zero and one. When the value is zero, it means that the actual income distribution is identical to the absolute fair distribution of income (perfect equality), where all the points of the distribution will fall on a 45° line. When the value is equal to one, it means that the income distribution is concentrated in one person or family. This means that when the value is closer to zero, income distribution will be nearer to a fair distribution. For more details, see Abu Shokor, A.F.: "Social Structure and Pattern of Income Distribution in the West Bank and Gaza Strip" (Nablus: An-Najah National University, January 1987, unpublished).

2. Michael Bohnet and Rupert Betz: *Einkommensverteilung in Entwicklungslaendern* (Munich, 1976), p. 25.

3. Ibid.

4. Ibid.

5. The unemployment rate is the percentage of unemployed among the active labor force (no. of unemployed + no. of employed). This definition does not include underemployment or seasonal unemployment. The latter type is widespread in the West Bank and Gaza Strip: if it is taken into consideration, the rate of unemployment reaches 36.71%. In the West Bank alone it reaches 37.57% and in the

Gaza Strip 33.90%. For more details, see Abu Shokor, A.F.: "Labor Market in the West Bank and Gaza Strip" (Nablus: An-Najah National University, February 1987, unpublished).

6. Additional work in the Israeli labor market means the head of household or a family member works part time there.

7. Abu Shokor: "Social Structure."

8. Ibid.

9. Ibid.

10. Ibid.

11. ibid.

12. Bassam K. Saket (supervisor): *Workers Migration Abroad: Socio-Economic Implications for Households in Jordan* (Amman: Royal Scientific Society, 1983), p. 132.

13. *Statistical Abstract of Israel, 1983* (Jerusalem: Central Bureau of Statistics, 1983), p. 78.

14. Abu Shokor: "Social Structure."

15. Ibid. p. 48.

16. Abu Shokor, A.F.: *Social and Economic Conditions of the Workers of the West Bank and Gaza Strip in Israel* (Nablus: An-Najah National University, April 1987), pp. 34-42.

17. Abu Shokor: "Social Structure."

18. Sarah Roy: *The Gaza Strip Survey* (Jerusalem: West Bank Data Base Project, Jerusalem 1986), p. 85.

19. Abu Shokor: "Social Structure."

20. Ibid. pp. 34-37.

21. Ibid.

22. *Statistical Abstract of Israel, 1978* (Jerusalem: Central Bureau of Statistics, 1978), p. 725.

23. Ibid.

24. Abu Shokor: "Social Structure."

25. Ibid. pp. 42.

26. This has been especially true since the *intifada* started in December 1987. From an economic point of view the *intifada* might lead to more polarization with respect to the social class structure. This process is enhanced by Israeli anti-*intifada* economic policies, which include an increased tax burden imposed on some income groups and measures to cut off residents in the West Bank and Gaza Strip from foreign financial funds such as remittances of migrant workers.

Bibliography

Abu Shokor, A.F.: "Social Structure and Pattern of Income Distribution in the West Bank and Gaza Strip." Nablus: An-Najah National University, January 1987, un-published.

_____: "Labor Market in the West Bank and Gaza Strip." Nablus: An-Najah National University, February 1987, unpublished.

_____: *Social and Economic Conditions of the Workers of the West Bank and Gaza*

Strip in Israel. Nablus: An-Najah National University, April 1987.

Benvenisti, Meron: *Demographic, Economic, Legal, Social and Political Developments in the West Bank: 1986 Report.* Boulder, Colo.: Westview Press, 1986.

Bohnet, Michael, and Betz, Rupert: *Einkommensverteilung in Entwicklungslaendern.* Munich, 1976.

Central Bureau of Statistics: *Statistical Abstract of Israel, 1978.* Jerusalem: Central Bureau of Statistics, 1978.

_____: *Statistical Abstract of Israel, 1983.* Jerusalem: Central Bureau of Statistics, 1983.

Foxley, Alejandro: *Income Distribution in Latin America.* London, 1976.

Metzer, J., Orth, M., and Sterzing, C.: *Das ist unser Land: West Bank and Gaza Streifen unter Israelischer Besatzung.* Bornheim-Merten, 1980.

Roy, Sara: *The Gaza Strip Survey.* Jerusalem: West Bank Data Base Project, 1986.

Saket, Bassam K., Al-Tell,Tariq, Zreigat, Sami, and Asfour, Bassam : *Workers Migration Abroad: Socio-Economic Implications for Households in Jordan.* Amman: Royal Scientific Society, 1983.

PART THREE

Policy Issues

8

The Poverty Line in Jordan

Mohammad Al-Saqour

1. Conceptual Overview

According to one of the reports by the International Labor Organization, the number of people in the world living below the poverty line rose in the period 1980-1985 by 1 million every month. By the year 2000, those below the poverty line may amount to 25% of the total world population unless corrective measures are adopted immediately. I paraphrase the words of the English philosopher John Donne in saying, "The death of any person takes away a part of me because I am a part of humanity."

Any attempt to give a picture of poverty and poverty lines must define poverty, the types of poverty, and the degrees of poverty; must define poverty lines for each type and their geographic distribution between urban and rural societies; and must link these definitions to the basic human needs that have to be satisfied. Sociologists maintain that poverty exists in every society, although in varying degrees according to time and locality. It is a social indicator reflecting the status of the underprivileged classes in a society in comparison with other classes in the same society. Thus, poverty is a humanitarian problem faced by all societies from the beginning of time and one that will continue to demand solutions in the future.

A working definition of poverty should be linked to the basic needs of the individual and the family that have to be met to an acceptable level. These include material needs, such as food and housing, and nonmaterial needs, such as entertainment and participation. Defining poverty is all the more difficult as poverty has no constant definition because of the interaction of economic, social, and political factors that make up the definition and influence it.

Nevertheless, the following definition of poverty meets the satisfaction of most sociologists and Islamic scholars: Poverty is defined in Islam as need, lack, and deprivation. The poor are those whose backs are metaphorically broken by their humiliation and destitution. This definition covers people who have no money or income and those whose income does not satisfy their needs or those of their families. Hence, the real criterion that defines poverty is satisfaction. Sociologists define poverty as the situation in which income is not sufficient to meet basic needs.

Before moving on to discuss the poverty line, let me define four funda-mental concepts. *Basic needs* are the needs necessary to preserve the individual's life at a certain level that protects his or her dignity and ability to work and earn. These needs include food and drink, clothes, housing, and educational achievement. Basic needs can be divided into nutritional needs, which include food and drink, and nonnutritional needs, which include housing, education, and health care.

Destitution is the state in which the basic nutritional needs are not satisfied--that is, when the individual does not consume the quantity of calories necessary to maintain life (2150-2200 calories per person per day). Consequently, the dividing line between those who consume the minimum quantity of calories and those who do not is called the destitution line.

Absolute poverty is the state in which the basic needs, nutritional as well as nonnutritional, are not met. The dividing line between those who satisfy their basic needs and those who do not is called the absolute poverty line.

Relative poverty is the proportion of poor people in a society and their standard of living compared with those of the more fortunate in the same society.

There are many schools of thought and many approaches that deal with the various types of poverty lines. Some draw a national poverty line that includes destitute and absolute poverty through the calculation of national averages. This chapter will not define a national poverty line by means of which all families and groups in Jordan can be categorized, although the chapter will refer to such a division and calculate some relevant national averages. Instead, the chapter will define several poverty lines so as to identify families that are incapable of meeting their recognized basic needs. In doing so, it is important to distinguish among the size of families, the age of their members, and their social and professional levels because the lines of relative poverty, absolute poverty, and even destitution, vary not only with respect to time and region within the same society but also from one family to another family living in the same street.

It is also necessary to specify the numerical indicators that identify and measure the poverty line and thus the level of poverty. Poverty can be measured by means of one indicator, such as fixed income. Alternatively, poverty can be measured by means of a combination of indicators, such as the economic and social standard of living and the level of consumption.

2. Identification of Types and Lines of Poverty

In selecting a measure of poverty from these concepts, we are wise to rely on the concepts of destitution and absolute poverty. Too many difficulties arise in measuring relative poverty, such as the difficulty of selecting appropriate criteria and the difficulty of conducting a study to measure relative poverty. In measuring destitution and absolute poverty, we have a wide range of indicators to select from once the criteria have been identified. These indicators include the minimum level necessary to satisfy basic nutritional needs, the minimum level necessary to satisfy basic nutritional as well as nonnutritional needs, and the levels of income and expenditure that may be assumed to satisfy the above mentioned needs.

The first criterion depends on designing various indicators that meet various needs. Consequently, this may be more appropriate for the purposes of planning and follow-up on development programs that aim to satisfy basic needs. Opinions also abound on the unit of measurement of poverty. Many economists maintain that the individual is an appropriate unit of measurement because many development indicators aim at the individual by sex, economic activity, and level of education. Others believe the family should be the measuring unit, given the difficulty of identifying the income level of every individual in the family, particularly in family-run business enterprises. This chapter will use both units of measurement, the individual and the family, to define the poverty line on the national and regional levels and to define the mobile poverty lines for each family.

3. Definition of the Destitution Line

Many factors control family expenditure on basic nutritional needs. Prime among these are the individual's needs for energy and other nutrients, the size of the family, the age distribution of its members, and the sex and the state of health of each member. Because there is a lack of data on basic needs specific to the kingdom, which vary with the environment and social norms,[1] the minimum calorie intake necessary to sustain life will be taken from a study conducted in Jordan using the levels of calorie intake recommended by the International Food and Agriculture Organization and the World Health Organization.

Table 8.1 compares the average expenditure on various food items as a proportion of total expenditure on food in Jordan and in the United States. The table shows that expenditure on meat and eggs constitutes one-third of the overall expenditure on food and that expenditure on sugar and sweets is very high, although such foodstuffs contain little nutritional value.

TABLE 8.1

Food Item Expenditure as a Proportion of Total Food Expenditure, Jordan and the United States

| Food Items | % of Total Expenditure on Food | |
	Jordan	United States
Cereals	12.5	11.9
Meat, eggs, and fish	30.3	38.8
Milk and dairy products	6.6	13.1
Fruits and vegetables	19.5	14.4
Oils and fats	12.4	3.4
Sugar, sweets, and soft drinks	14.2	7.0
Other processed materials	4.5	11.4
Total	100%	100%

Sources: Department of Statistics, *Price Section--1987 series* (Amman, n.d.); United States Department of Agriculture, *Survey, 1977-1978* (Washington, D.C.: US Government Printing Office, 1979).

The study on Pockets of Poverty in Jordan currently being conducted by the Ministry of Social Development,[2] calculated the cost of certain food baskets according to current prices and the geographical location of individuals and families as well as the cost of the food basket for an individual and a family. Table 8.2 shows the average cost in Jordan for the

TABLE 8.2

Monthly Family Expenditure on Nutritional Needs According to Geographical Location and Family Size, 1987 [a]

| Geographic Location (governorate) | Family Size (F) | Monthly Average Expenditure (JD) | |
		Individual (P)	Family (FxP)
Amman	6.94	5.628	39.060
Irbid	7.28	5.572	40.567
Balqa	7.98	5.581	44.537
Karak	8.42	5.616	47.287
Ma'an	7.72	5.865	45.279
Zarqa	7.10	5.659	40.820
Mafraq	7.72	5.565	42.963
Tafileh	7.16	5.662	40.545
National average	7.20	5.619	40.461

[a] Current prices.

Source: Ministry of Social Development, *Pockets of Poverty in Jordan, 1987* (forthcoming).

food baskets based on average family size, and geographical location.

The table shows that a Jordanian individual's monthly nutritional needs cost JD 5.619 on average, at 1987 prices. Given that the average family in the Hashemite Kingdom of Jordan consists of 7.20 members, the minimum expenditure required to satisfy the family's basic nutritional needs is JD 40.461 per month. In Amman governorate, JD 39.060 is needed to purchase the least expensive food basket. The highest cost of nutritional needs is in Karak governorate (JD 47.278), followed by Ma'an.

Therefore, when calculating poverty lines, if we assume that each family has its own poverty line when only the size of the family is taken into consideration, the destitution line for any family in any governorate in Jordan is the product of the family size and the average monthly expenditure per individual for that governorate.

Number of family members times price of food basket per individual is destitution line: F x P = Destitution line.

If a family in Ma'an has four members, the destitution line for that family lies at the 4 x 5.865 = 23.460 dinars per month mark.

More accurate figures for the destitution line can be calculated by considering variables other than family size, such as sex, age, or pregnancy, as shown in Table 8.3.

If we calculate the destitution line using the number of members in the family, their age groups, sex (for those older than thirteen), and the number of women who are pregnant or breastfeeding, we will get greater accuracy in defining both the price of the food basket and the poverty line,

TABLE 8.3
Minimum Price of Basic Monthly Nutritional needs According to Age, Sex, Pregnancy, and Breastfeeding

Age Group (years)	Price of the Individual Monthly Food Basket (JD)	
less than 1	3.190	
01-06	3.540	
07-09	4.820	
10-12	5.400	
	Males	Females
13-60	6.210	5.650
61 and more	5.460	5.150
Pregnant and breastfeeding cases		6.700

Source: Ministry of Social Development, *Pockets of Poverty in Jordan, 1987* (forthcoming).

which will vary from one family to another and sometimes from one region to another.

Therefore, there is no general national destitution line; there are destitution lines that vary from one family to another. For instance, a family consisting of a father, a pregnant mother, a child younger than six, and another aged ten who attends school would have its destitution line at the JD 21.850 per month mark.

4. Definition of the Absolute Poverty Line

The various factors that govern the satisfaction of the basic nutritional and nonnutritional needs of the individual and the family define and control the absolute poverty line. The basic nutritional needs can be well defined and translated into a financial equivalent. Nonnutritional needs are not easily defined, however. Moreover, these needs are constantly increasing in quality and quantity, and they vary with respect to region and period of time. The calculation becomes yet more difficult when it comes to translating these needs into financial equivalents or when it comes to considering the family, as opposed to the individual, as the unit of measurement. The situation is further exacerbated when the economist attempts to combine the two units (the individual and the family) into one formula. Generally speaking, such calculations require high technical expertise and detailed data that are not available in Jordan.

For the purpose of this chapter, basic needs are defined as the following:

1. Food: The food requirement of the individual and family necessary to sustain life translated into a financial value.
2. Housing: The minimal adequate housing arrangement.
3. Clothing and shoes: The minimum requirements of family members.
4. Education: The minimum expenditure necessary to cover educational needs at the compulsory stage in Jordan.
5. Health: The minimum expenditure necessary to pay for the health services needed in Jordan.
6. Transportation: The minimum expenditure needed to cover transportation needs.

The preliminary result of the Pockets of Poverty in Jordan study of 1987 and of the Household Expenditure surveys conducted by the Department of Statistics in 1980 and 1986 [3] show how the average family budget is spent on basic nutritional and nonnutritional needs as defined here. On average, 45.5% of the family budget at the absolute poverty line is spent on nutritional needs, and 54.5% is spent on basic nonnutritional needs.

Therefore, the average cost of the minimum basic nonnutritional needs of the Jordanian family is 48.460 per month for an average family of 7.2 members. The cost of the minimum nutritional needs is JD 40.460. Thus, the minimum required to meet the minimum monthly nutritional and basic nonnutritional needs of an average family of 7.2 members is JD 89 (48.460 + 40.460 = 88.920). More details can be found in Table 8.4, which is taken from the preliminary data of the Pockets of Poverty Survey.

Identification of the poverty line at the macrolevel follows the same methodology as at the microlevel. The absolute poverty line for an average Jordanian family is JD 89, but each family has a line that depends on its size, the sex of its members, their age, and level at school. These are linked by means of an algebraic formula with constants and variables. In the case of basic nonnutritional needs, the minimum cost of health, transportation, and clothes and shoes is assumed to be constant and is given a single cost value regardless of family size, age, and sex. As for education and housing, they are assumed to vary with the family size, and they are calculated as part of the JD 89 figure on the basis of the average Jordanian family. Consequently, the poverty line varies from the JD 89 monthly mark according to the size of the family and the condition and sex of its members.

5. Institutions for the Assistance of the Poor

Jordan has achieved considerable progress in providing the services that cater to the citizen's basic nonnutritional needs. In the early 1970s, a new approach to social work was adopted that linked welfare and rehabilitation programs with the less privileged section of society. The early 1980s saw a noticeable rise in the number of social welfare funds that helped the poor and dealt with the problems of poverty and the underprivileged.

5.1 The Institutions

There are four public and private institutions that provide assistance to the poor.

5.1.1 The National Aid Fund (NAF)

The NAF was established in October 1986 as an organization of the Ministry of Social Development with financial and administrative autonomy and with two main objectives: to protect and assist needy families by giving them financial assistance on a monthly basis and in emergencies and to raise the income of individuals and families by giving them opportunities

TABLE 8.4
Absolute Poverty Line for an Average Jordanian Family, 1987

Expense	% of Budget	Average Monthly Cost [a]	
		Individual	Family
Basic nutritional needs	45.5	5.620	40.500
Basic non-nutritional needs			
Housing	32.0	4.000	28.400
Education	3.9	0.480	3.500
Health	2.0	0.250	1.800
Clothes	7.8	0.970	7.000
Transportation	8.8	1.080	7.800
Total	100.0	12.400	89.000

[a] Cost in JD, based on January 1988 prices.

Source : Ministry of Social Development, *Pockets of Poverty in Jordan, 1987* (forthcoming).

to be productive through physical and vocational rehabilitation programs.

The NAF was established as an alternative to the Cash Assistance and the Rehabilitation Section of the ministry, which functioned in the same way as the NAF. The only difference in the working of the two institutions has been the rise in allocations for the poor from JD 1.5 million in 1986 to JD 3.0 million in 1987 as well as the financial and administrative autonomy of the fund. The NAF is directed by a board chaired by the minister of social development and includes two members representing the other funds that work in the same field and representatives from the General Union of Voluntary Societies, the Ministry of Health, the Vocational Training Corporation, the Noor Al-Hussein Foundation, and the Queen Alia Fund for Social Work.

The NAF budget in 1987 was JD 4.12 million, which was disbursed as follows:

Monthly recurrent donations	84.1%
Vocational rehabilitation assistance	12.8%
Physical rehabilitation assistance	2.4%
Emergency assistance	0.7%

The NAF derives its income from the allocations of the Ministry of Finance, which come from the social services tax.

5.1.2 The Zakah Fund (ZF)

The ZF was founded by means of a special law in 1978 as an institution with administrative and financial autonomy working to alleviate the suffering of the poor, the destitute, the needy, and those working to spread the teachings of Islam by providing them with regular and emergency assistance as well as through physical and vocational rehabilitation programs. The ZF is directed by a board chaired by the minister of *Awqaf* and Islamic affairs and holy places and comprising representatives from the NAF and private sector bodies. The income of the ZF is derived from the *zakah* (alms) and other donations. In 1988 the ZF achieved a major breakthrough in the services it offered, in comparison with the previous year, when its total income reached JD 276,000. Regular donations make up 78% of the ZF budget, emergency assistance 5.4%, and social programs 16.6%. The main difference between the ZF and the NAF is that the NAF derives its income from the treasury (the total social service tax collected, plus JD 75,000 from the General Union of Voluntary Societies), whereas the ZF relies on private donation. The other major difference is that the NAF provides assistance to Jordanians only, while the ZF also provides assistance to non-Jordanian Muslims among others.

5.1.3 Private Zakah Committees

These committees were formed on a voluntary basis in all villages and neighborhoods of the kindom. In 1982 there were thirty-eight such committees licensed to receive *zakah* from people in their localities and disburse them to the poor in that locality. Private donations constitute the main source of income of these committees and include collections at mosques, which account for 13% of the committees' income; *adahi* (meat donated by Muslims for distribution to the poor), which accounts for 13% of the committees' income; and foreign sources--some committees are able to attract donations from Arab and foreign sources.

Zakah committees provide various services. In 1988, these included regular financial donations, which reached a total of JD 99,625 and were distributed to 790 families; emergency financial assistance, which was given to 200 families; physical and vocational rehabilitation assistance, which was dispensed to a varying number of families (2 to 25 for any one committee); and donations for health care and medicine, which also varied (2 to 550 families per committee). Table 8.5 shows in greater detail an analysis of *zakah* committees according to the type of assistance they give and the average number of families they help.

5.1.4 Voluntary Organizations (Charities)

There are 450 voluntary organization in Jordan [4] that offer the following

TABLE 8.5
Zakah Committee Services, 1987

Type of Service	Annual Budget (JD)	Families Served	Average Donation (JD)	No. of Committees	% of Committees [a]
Monthly regular	60-99,625	1-790	0.33-15.8	26	84.0
Emergency aid	40-7,731	0-200	4-100	18	58.0
Gifts of Food, etc.	150-20,000	14-550	3-80	18	58.0
Physical rehabilitation	60-300	1-7	43-90	6	19.5
Vocational rehabilitation	90-1,750	2-25	18-875	7	23.0
Health/medicine	50-10,000	2-550	4-150	12	39.0
Other	38-5,153	2-100	14-172	12	39.0

[a] In 1987, the total number of licensed private zakah committees was 31.

Source: Ministry of Social Development, *Pockets of Poverty in Jordan, 1987* (forthcoming).

services:

- Monthly financial aid to individuals and families of the locality given with the approval of the members of the organization; the smallest number of families served by any one organization is 1 and the largest is 425.
- Emergency financial assistance, which ranges from JD 4 to JD 450 for a single case.
- Physical and vocational rehabilitation assistance, which is receiving more and more attention.
- Assistance for health care and medicine; the money offered for one case ranges from JD 1 to JD 200.

5.2 Standards of Operation

There is agreement among the four agencies that offer assistance to the poor concerning the standards by which they operate. These standards are as follows:

1. The family is the basic unit.
2. Families with a total monthly income lower than a fixed limit of JD 20 to JD 40 (it varies among agencies) for a family of five can apply for regular monthly financial assistance.
3. Families with a total monthly income of less than JD 80 can apply for rehabilitation assistance.
4. Families may qualify for assistance in cases in which the head of the household has a very low income or suffers from poor health such

that his or her ability to work is reduced by 60%.

5. Families can apply for assistance if the head of the household is absent, under arrest, or dead and there is no other adult who can look after the family.

Assistance is offered only after a social study has been conducted to identify the level of need. It should be noted that the private voluntary organizations often give assistance to families on a regular basis without adherence to these standards after members of the committee or organization have approved a request from a member of their community.

6. Conclusion

Poverty has become an obvious phenomenon during the current recession in Jordan. So far, poverty has not led to serious negative developments in related social dimensions due to the conservative nature of Jordanian society and to the firm social ties that subsist among members of this society. Nevertheless, the problems associated with poverty and the poor will become more serious unless the economic performance of Jordan improves and unless policies are implemented to deal with these problems. Population growth continues at the high rate of 3.5% or more, and every year now not less than 30,000 workers including graduates enter the job market. If these numbers are not absorbed, unemployment will increase and with it the poverty level in the country.

Notes

1. Dr. Salma Touqan and Mashour Al-Shunnaq: "Report to the 'Pockets of Poverty in Jordan' Study Project" (1987, unpublished).

2. Ministry of Social Development, *Pockets of Poverty in Jordan, 1987* (forthcoming).

3. Department of Statistics: *Family Expenditure Survey, 1980* (Amman, n.d.); Department of Statistics: *Household Expenditure and Income Survey, 1986-1987* (Amman, n.d.).

4. The General Union of Voluntary Societies is the official representative of most of those organizations in the kingdom.

Bibliography

Department of Statistics: *Family Expenditure Survey, 1980*. Amman, n.d.
_____: *Household Expenditure and Income Survey, 1986-1987.* Amman,n.d.
_____: *Price Section--1987 Series*. Amman, n.d.
Ministry of Social Development: *Pockets of Poverty in Jordan*. Forthcoming.
Touqan, Salma and Al-Shunnaq, Mashour: "Report to the 'Pockets of Poverty in

Jordan' Study Project." Amman, 1987, unpublished.
United States Department of Agriculture: *Survey, 1977-1978.* Washington, D.C.:
    United States Government Printing Office, 1979.

9

Social Security Scheme and Income Distribution

Ghassan Musallam

It has always required more imagination to apprehend reality than to ignore it.
— J. Giraudoux

1. Introduction

The title of this chapter implies that the subject of income distribution should be tackled in terms of the relationship between social security contributions/benefits and their effects on income distribution in a given economy. The available literature, however, tends to emphasize social security retirement annuities and their implications as far as national savings and individual welfare are concerned in the presence of capital market imperfections.

One of the aims of a social security old-age pension scheme is to maintain consumption in retirement. An actuarially fair social security scheme can generate substantial increases in lifetime consumption and welfare improvements where there is uncertainty about longevity and a private annuity market is imperfect or absent. Nevertheless, social security schemes normally reduce other individual savings and affect behaviour during the whole life cycle, not just in old age. Compulsory contributions put constraints on individuals' cash flow and in the presence of restrictions on borrowing and the interaction of higher steady-state interest rates offset the gains obtained by the introduction of a social security scheme.[1] This chapter is an attempt to examine the relationship between a social security scheme and a certain number of macroeconomic variables in order to discover new approaches to the role of a social security scheme in a country such as Jordan.

A certain number of issues regarding income distribution should be clarified. Although income distribution indicates the flow of wealth within a society, the main concern of research should be with changes in income distribution rather than income distribution itself--that is, with whether it is an accurate measure of productivity or of welfare. If income is a measure of productivity, market forces can affect the relationship between production factors. It is difficult to isolate labor, capital, and technology from one another due to the complementarity existing among them. When income is a measure of welfare, differentials in income will indicate differentials in the command of goods and services. In this context, the basis of the indicator is the family, not the individual. But methodological problems arise, especially in developing countries, for as the income of a family increases, children and women spend more time in full-time education and enter the labor market later or opt for nonremunerated jobs. Nonmonetary income introduces another dimension into the assessment of income distribution as a measure of welfare. The assumption that welfare is affected by the number of persons in a family unit (hence the necessity to use income per capita as a measure) does not take account of the fact that cultural and/or religious beliefs related to fecundity are of primary value and supercede material goods.

Income distribution changes continuously as it is subject to both economic and market forces. Economic changes and the development of more sophisticated organized societies have enhanced the creation of pressure groups. Employees, employers, moneylenders (banks) and others, nonhomogeneous groups, and more or less organized groups have introduced a continual, open negotiation among different bodies to adjust income distribution levels. The existence of these groups modifies the structure of the labor and capital markets determining the remuneration of production factors. The government acts as an arbitrator aimed at establishing a consensus about income distribution.

2. The Jordanian Social Security Scheme

The primary objective of this chapter is to lead the reader to an understanding of the role, function, and future of the Jordanian social security scheme and what it entails in terms of benefits and costs. The current scheme is in its eighth year at the time of this writing, and the experience acquired is under scrutiny. Any analysis is merely preliminary for the simple reason that a scheme is mature only thirty to forty years after its institution.

Actuarial studies, undertaken periodically, measure the financial soundness of the social security scheme, given a set of obligations and benefits, and propose policies regarding the financing of such a scheme. The social security scheme in Jordan is a self-financed one in which every generation tries to finance and cover costs pertaining to the expected benefits. The following are the major features of the scheme.

2.1 Available Data

The Social Security Corporation was established in 1979. Thus far, it has registered more than 430,000 workers. To understand this figure, it is important to differentiate among active members, suspended members, and beneficiaries.

The most significant operational term is *active members*--those who pay contributions. The term *suspended members* refers to those who were active members at one time but who for one reason or another are no longer contributing to the scheme. The term *beneficiaries* refers to those receiving short- or long-term or lump-sum benefits; beneficiaries are included in the number previously mentioned.

The number of active members increased from 37,320 in 1980 to 237,121 in 1986, as shown in Table 9.1.

Non-Jordanians represented 13.9% of the total number of active members in 1980. This percentage had increased to 24.58% by 1986. This rise in the proportion of non-Jordanians stemmed from the extension of the scheme to cover private sector companies that employ five persons or more.

In 1986, the age distribution of active members compared to the age distribution of the population of Jordan was as listed in Table 9.2.

There are several striking features to this table. The modal age group of female and male, affiliated population is twenty to twenty-four years, followed by the twenty-five to twenty-nine age group. More than 57% of the female, active, affiliated population belong to the age group of twenty to twenty-nine, in comparison with less than 39% in the male, affiliated population. The relatively low percentage of contributors in the fifteen to nineteen age group is explained by the fact that many members of this age group are still in full-time secondary education.

Two figures are particularly interesting: 863 women of sixty years or more are working, although the retirement age is fifty-five years, and 9,656 men older than sixty, are also still working, that is 6.4% of the active members of the scheme, although the retirement age is sixty. This situation may be the result of particular social or economic factors, but a

TABLE 9.1
Active Contributors to Social Security, 1980-1986

Contributors	1980	1981	1982	1983	1984	1985	1986
Jordanians	32,117	99,001	130,370	138,798	162,316	171,656	178,832
Non-Jordanians	5,203	22,355	45,509	51,566	59,566	59,415	58,289
Total	37,320	121,356	175,879	190,364	221,882	231,071	237,121

Source: Social Security Corporation.

TABLE 9.2
Active Social Security Members and Jordanian Population by Age Group, 1986

	Female				Male			
	Estimated Population		Active Members		Estimated Population		Active Members	
Age Group	Number	%	Number	%	Number	%	Number	%
15-19	159,900	24.5	3,237	11.3	178,400	24.6	7,701	5.1
20-24	119,800	18.3	10,461	36.5	134,600	18.6	29,530	19.7
25-29	81,300	12.5	5,916	20.6	92,100	12.7	28,419	18.9
30-34	61,300	9.3	2,558	8.9	67,300	9.3	17,357	11.7
35-39	56,100	8.5	2,114	7.7	58,500	8.1	13,872	9.2
40-44	50,700	7.8	1,489	5.2	55,600	7.7	14,451	9.6
45-49	42,600	6.5	1,174	4.1	49,700	6.8	12,661	8.4
50-54	36,000	5.5	651	2.3	39,500	5.4	10,219	6.8
55-59	26,600	4.0	190	0.7	29,300	4.0	6,313	4.2
60-64	18,700	3.0	863	3.0	20,400	2.8	9,656	6.4
Total	653,000	100.0	28,653	100.0	725,400	100.0	150,179	100.0

Source: Department of Statistics, Statistical Yearbook, 1987 (Amman, n.d.); and Social Security Corporation.

special study would be necessary to identify the socioeconomic conditions that encourage men and women to remain in employment beyond retirement age.

Imperfections in the collection of these statistical data should not be entirely discounted. One possible explanation for why these individuals work beyond retirement could be a combination of social attitudes and human capital theory: Males are expected to be lifetime earners, but they invest in their education more intensively than do women, thereby delaying their entry into professional life.

Another aspect of considerable economic significance is the total value of monthly wages of contributors. The total value of wages subject to contributions increased from JD 58.47 million in 1980 to JD 349.8 million in 1986. The average monthly wages of contributors in the years 1980 and 1986 respectively are shown in Table 9.3.

The average wage of Jordanians contributing to the scheme decreased throughout the period, the main reason for this decrease being the affiliation to the scheme of workers in small firms and civil servants not covered under the Civil Pension Law, most of whom are paid less than JD 100 per month.

Average wages for non-Jordanians contributing to the scheme increased. One of the determinant factors of this increase is the affiliation of expatriates working in Jordan on a contractual basis with Jordanian and

TABLE 9.3
Average Monthly Wages of Social Security Contributors, 1980 and 1986 (JD)

Contributors	1980	1986
Jordanian males	141.0	131.7
Non-Jordanian males	89.0	112.0
Jordanian females	102.0	97.7
Non-Jordanian females	93.7	129.0

Source: Social Security Corporation.

foreign establishments. Further analysis is needed to relate average wages to educational background or position of affiliates in order fully to understand income distribution. The processing of the available data to obtain income distribution of all contributors had not been completed at the time of this writing.

The preceding data reflect the following situation:

1. In 1986, the total value of wages of contributors to the scheme amounted to 47 % of the total of wages and salaries in Jordan.
2. The number of affiliates in 1986 was nearly 237,121 representing 45% of the total work force in Jordan.
3. Average wages in Jordan in 1986 were around JD 120 per month compared to an average of JD 123 for those who were affiliated. Taking into consideration possible statistical inconsistencies (sources regarding wages in 1986: Royal Scientific Society, Social Security Corporation, Department of Statistics), these two averages are very close to each other, although it is still difficult to assert that income distribution of the affiliated population is similar to that of the country as a whole.
4. The average monthly wage per affiliated male worker (Jordanian and non-Jordanian) in 1986 was JD 126.400 compared to the average monthly wage of JD 122.300 for all male workers in Jordan.[2] The average monthly wage per affiliated female worker in the same year was JD 100.500 compared to the average monthly wage of JD 110.400 for all female workers in Jordan.

These results and comparisons are not significant for the simple reason that wages subject to contributions are different from those published in the aforementioned sources. In fact, not all the components of wages are included when contributions are assessed; for example, overtime payments and transportation allowances are not included.

A comparative study of wages by field of activity (sector), age group, and educational background will be possible once computarization is finalized (all relevant data electronically processed). A comparative study of wages by age group between the study population and the total Jordanian labor force is necessary to admit statistically that those affiliated to the scheme are a representative sample of the labor force in all respects.

2.2 Sources of Funds

The pension scheme is basically self-financed; contributions are borne by employers and employees. The employer's share of contributions amounts to 8% of the total payroll, and the employee's share is 5% of salary. The employer has sole responsibility for financing the industrial accident and occupational diseases scheme at a rate of 2% of wages and salaries.

As shown in Table 9.4, contributions increased throughout the period 1980-1987. This was due to the extension of coverage: More and more economic sectors were affiliated to the scheme, and coverage was progressively extended to include all institutions and companies employing five persons or more. Investment earnings progessed steadily and reached JD 11.316 million in 1987. This represented a return on investments of 6% per year, the highest since 1980.

The investment strategy is to maximize the real value of assets and to participate in the socioeconomic development of the kingdom. The prime objective, however, is to serve the scheme, ensure its future without having to increase the cost of contributions, and, if possible, increase the level of benefits.

As far as recovery of contributions is concerned, the scheme can claim that at least 80% of the contributions due are collected. In certain sectors, collection of contributions proves difficult for a variety of reasons; in other cases, there are cash flow problems, which explains why some of the establishments affiliated to the scheme are in arrears on payments.

2.3 Social Security Benefits

A short summary of the existing benefits will give a clear picture of the

TABLE 9.4
Sources of Social Security Funds, 1980-1987 (million JD)

Sources	1980	1981	1982	1983	1984	1985	1986	1987
Contributions	4.753	11.581	23.988	27.360	36.440	38.702	45.459	44.100
Return on investments	0.105	0.563	1.538	2.909	4.017	3.878	8.177	11.300
Total	4.858	12.144	25.526	30.269	40.457	42.580	53.636	55.400

Source: Social Security Corporation.

nature of coverage offered by the Jordanian social security scheme. Some of these benefits, such as lump-sum compensation for partial disability or medical insurance against industrial accidents, are proposed and secured by insurance companies in Jordan. Other benefits, such as the minimum pension and the survivors' pension, are not available on the open market, and profit-oriented insurance companies are not in a position to guarantee such benefits.

The benefits can be divided into four groups. *Pensions* are disbursed for disability resulting from industrial accident, old age, or natural disability. *Survivor pensions* are disbursed in case of death resulting from an accident at work or death from natural causes. *Lump-sum compensations* are disbursed for industrial accidents or partial disability (less than 30%). *Withdrawal lump-sum compensations* are disbursed to those cashing in their benefits in the scheme (for example, on marriage, emigration, or departure from the country of non-Jordanian workers). Table 9A.1 illustrates the nature of the scheme: coverage, qualifying conditions, and benefits.

Qualifying conditions for benefits are as follows: The retirement age is sixty years for men and fifty-five for women, with a minimum of ten consecutive years of contribution or fifteen nonconsecutive years. Early retirement is possible for those who reach the age of forty-six and have made full contribution for at least fifteen years. If an employee has an industrial accident, then occupational diseases benefits (medical expenses and daily allowances) are payable from the first day of activity and affiliations. Medical committees examine cases to determine the level of disability and hence the corresponding compensation. Rehabilitation services are totally covered by the scheme.

Beneficiaries and benefits can be characterized as follows (also see Table 9A.1): By December 31, 1987, pensions were payable to 3,801 persons and their families. In 1986, the total value of pensions paid was JD 2.584 million compared with JD 1.779 million in 1985. These payments represented 0.26% and 0.35% of total wages for 1985 and 1986, respectively; contributions represented almost 15% of the total wages bill for insured workers. These ratios were only 3% and 2.49% for 1985 and 1986, respectively, if all benefits payments and administrative costs were considered.

These figures representing the outflow, per month or per year, should be compared to the inflow stipulated by the law as 15% of total wages. The comparison indicates that substantial surpluses are accumulated (investable funds), thereby securing a sound long term future for the system. From an actuarial point of view, there is a deficit when annual outflow (total benefit payment and administrative costs) is higher than the annual inflow. In other words, when monthly contributions during the course of one year no longer cover the annual expenses for the scheme, the system has still income generated from investments and at a later stage can utilize surpluses accumulated during previous years to honor its liabilities. A certain number of solutions should be studied to balance outflows and inflows--for example, higher rates of contributions and/or restriction of benefits and qualifying conditions. Encouragingly, the preliminary results of the 1986 actuarial projection indicated an inflow covering outflow for the next forty-five years.

The number of pensioners by age and survivors is increasing; it rose from 936 persons in 1984 to 1,660 persons in 1987. The number of natural disability pensioners almost doubles every year. Cases are examined by the medical committee. The concept of disability as expressed and stipulated by the law is restrictive: A disabled person is someone who cannot make a living out of any job at all. In practical terms, the concept has evolved, and there is now a more flexible understanding of natural disability. Given the relative newness of the scheme, most of those receiving natural disability pensions have an average of no more than seven years of contributions. The pension payable is equivalent to 50% of the last monthly wage.

Medical expenses and allowances stabilized in the period 1986-1987, but expenses per case increased during the same period. These overall results should be analyzed and tabulated in terms of medical expenses (hospitalization, number of beds/days, number of surgical operations) and all other relevant expenses. These totaled JD 2.6 million by the end of 1987.

Early termination benefits constitute a major item of benefit expenditure. By the end of 1987, the number of people who had claimed lump-sum compensation was 24,647 Jordanians, 31,290 Egyptians, and 15,857 people of other nationalities. The total value of lump-sum compensation paid out was by 1987 JD 19.67 million.

2.4 Social Security Pensions and Other Payments Until Maturity of the Scheme

Wages and salaries in the gross domestic product (GDP) witnessed an accelerated increase from 1975 to 1986, increasing from JD 120 million to JD 738 million (18% per annum). The Table 9.5 compares pensions with wages and salaries for the period 1980-1986.

Lump-sum compensations, temporary industrial accident allowances, and nonmonetary transfers (medical expenses and other related expenditure) will increase the share of social security payments in the volume of wages and salaries if these are considered to be benefits derived from wages and salaries. This share will increase from 0.05% in 1981 to 1.00%

TABLE 9.5
Pensions in Relation to Wages and Salaries, 1980-1986 (million JD)

	1980	1981	1982	1983	1984	1985	1986
Wages and salaries	410.000	474.000	550.000	604.000	650.000	689.000	738.000
Pensions		0.030	0.120	0.357	0.672	1.800	2.600
Ratio (%)			0.00	0.06	0.10	0.26	0.35

Source: Department of Statistics, *Statistical Yearbook 1987* (Amman, n.d.).

in 1986.

The significance of social security payments in wages and salaries is limited for the time being, but such payments are steadily increasing and at far higher rates than are wages and salaries in GDP. The relative newness of the scheme explains the rapid increase in the number of pensioners, in the total amount paid out (JD 6.6 million up to 1987), and in lump-sum compensations to Jordanians (JD 7.7 million up to 1987) and to non-Jordanians (JD 11.5 million up to 1987). The scheme will stabilize as it matures, when the rates of increase in the number of beneficiaries and in payments made will decelerate.

It is difficult to project what the share of pensions and other forms of transfers in the GDP in comparison to wages and salaries will be in the future. Nevertheless, an actuarial valuation, which should be performed periodically, has as its objective to ensure that financial equilibrium is achieved and that the stated aims of the scheme are consistent with actual experience.

The first actuarial review of the Jordanian scheme, which is a prospective one-hundred-year study with all its imperfections, does not give an appreciation of the role of the social security scheme in the national economy, but it does shed some light on areas of importance in evaluating the extent and nature of the financial obligations that the scheme will place on future generations after the provisions of the social security law become fully effective and the population matures. The review will also help to determine whether current provisions for financing the scheme will be adequate. The actuarial review calculates the long-term cash flow projection of both contributions and benefits arising from coverage, the cost of introducing a minimum pension rate, the effect of more stable economic conditions, the growth in the assets and liabilities of the scheme, and the organization of investment management and investment policy.

The main conclusions of the first actuarial review were as follows:

1. The existing contribution rate is sufficient to meet the cost of administration and benefit payments for a substantial period.

2. Substantial cash will be available for investment.
3. If pensions are revalued fully in line with increases in the cost of living, the existing contribution rate should be sufficient for fifty to sixty years. This is dependent on whether pensions are fully indexed or whether any increase in benefits is only to offset partially how inflation affects the purchasing power of benefits.
4. The long-term cost of introducing a minimum monthly pension rate is expected to be relatively insignificant.
5. A lenient claim procedure that would result in a significantly higher level of natural disability pensions is expected to increase costs by the equivalent of between 1% and 3% of monthly wages.
6. Projections indicate that when the scheme is fully mature in fifty to sixty years, the contribution cost may well be substantially higher than the existing contribution rate, given different rates of population growth.
7. Investment policy should concentrate on investments that minimize the "inflation risk"; investment returns should be closely monitored.

In terms of equity, there are strong arguments in favor of full "blanketing in" of those who were already over pension age at the commencement of the scheme and who therefore cannot benefit from it. It would seem, to say the least, ungenerous for those now of working age to promise themselves pensions at the expense of the next generation of earners if they are not prepared themselves to accept a similar responsibility for the generation already "blanketing in." This is not only equitable; it is also prudent.

2.5 Other Developments and Prospects

Social partners in the social security scheme are conveying interest in developing the coverage and benefits while minimizing possible cost. Trade unions are seeking more benefits for the affiliated in terms of allocations of surpluses to housing scheme mainly. Employers are looking to recycle a share of surpluses in their own ventures. Experience acquired in the application of the provisions of the law, however, and feedback received from all interested parties have raised a certain number of issues and possible developments.

2.5.1 Minimum Pension

The board of directors of the Social Security Corporation has decided on a minimum monthly pension of JD 30. This amount represents the pension to be disbursed to an insured person contributing for twenty-five years and getting a minimum salary of JD 60 per month. This minimum is granted to all persons qualifying for a pension regardless of the number of years of contributions and actual wage. This minimum is a synthetic income reflecting thinking on poverty and is considered to be a maintenance income (subsistence level). It is revised from time to time and is subject to any socioeconomic changes that may occur.

2.5.2 Extension of Coverage and Enforcement of Other Schemes

Coverage has been extended to all firms employing five persons and more. Voluntary affiliation is open to all Jordanians in the kingdom and abroad. Nevertheless, large sectors of the economy are not covered: the self-employed, farmers, and those who work in firms employing fewer than five persons. Experience has shown that the extension of coverage to small and medium size firms was not without problems or opponents. Employers see their liquidity shrinking, their businesses need time to adapt to regular disbursements, and contributions are considered an increase in direct labor costs. With encouragement, the system will cover all sectors. In this respect, close coordination between different professional associations and the Social Security Corporation will extend coverage to the self-employed, farmers, and other economic sectors.

Enforcement of *other insurances* (health, family allowances, unemployment) depends on prevailing economic conditions, reorganization of the provision of medical services, and broad government welfare strategy and policy. A fully fledged social security system is after all a judicious balance between costs (direct and social) and benefits. Social security costs in industrialized countries represent up to 45% of wages; benefits represent 20% to 22% of GDP.

According to tentative calculations, health insurance in Jordan cost 10% of all wages and salaries in 1987. Enforcement of a statutory health insurance scheme will create higher demands on medical services. Dynamic pressure on cost is to be expected and will push health insurance costs above 10% of all wages and salaries. The next crucial question concerns how social partners will cover the cost and in what proportions.

Unemployment benefit, as a recognized social demand, stems from the idea that the government is supposed to provide work for every person entering the labor market. This concept has led large sectors of the population to ask the concerned authorities to build up a compensation system for the unemployed, reinforcing the image of the state as a welfare state. But such an unemployment benefit scheme may be seen from two points of view, as a welfare measure or as an insurance scheme. In the former case the government and related bodies are mostly concerned with the insertion of newcomers into the labor market.

Certain monetary and nonmonetary aid is provided, the major group concerned being those entering the labor market on completion of their full-time education at any level or in any field. As an insurance scheme, there should be a fund financed by employees and employers to maintain a minimum income for those who have been obliged for various reasons-- such as sectoral difficulties and restructuring or closing down of firms--to leave their jobs. Benefits are generally dependent on the fulfilment of certain qualifying conditions that determine the type and duration of benefit entitlements. This system depends mostly on the common under-standing of social partners--government, employers, and employees-- whereas in the case of unemployment benefit as a welfare measure, the cost is borne by the state, and the major issue becomes the economic and financial capacity of the country to provide the necessary funds.

To summarize, the development of the present social security scheme into a fully fledged social insurance system forms part of a comprehensive policy to introduce integrated welfare and insurance systems, whereby a policy of revenue is defined and a system of redistribution of wealth is set up to secure a better redistribution of the fruits of economic development.

3. Conclusions

This chapter has briefly examined the nature of Jordan's social security scheme, its role, and its potential developments. The extension of cover-age, the introduction of new insurances, and the institution of a minimum pension may be considered by the legislator or by the government as tools for the implementation of redistribution and revenue policies.

But the discussion should be restricted to whether the desicionmaker will opt for these policies; the discussion must concern the ability of a given economy to finance such welfare programs. In developing countries a social security scheme and investment requirements (developing policy) can be detrimental to social policies. In some cases, the limited capacities of a particular administration for tax recovery and the financial difficulties and constraints caused by the creation of different insurance schemes (for the most needy of the population) constitute a handicap for any revenue redistribution (monetary and nonmonetary).

As a developing country, Jordan has adopted a broad-based social policy to ensure the population as a whole abides by the economic and social plan and to promote an acceptable level of redistribution of the fruits of the economic development of the country to all different social "classes" and regions. The relatively short experience of the implementation of socioeconomic policies regarding housing, health, education, and social welfare has been under scrutiny. The conclusions include that the mere juxtaposition of these different policies and consequent duplication of institutions providing similar services must be avoided. This thinking is also now being applied to similar cases of duplication in policies and institutions in some of the productive sectors. In light of this approach, redistribution policy (income redistribution) should be integrated into a general framework called the social budget of the nation.

3.1 Social Budget of the Nation

The concept of a social budget of the nation is a comprehensive approach to the problem of the citizen in his or her village or town dealing with his or her basic needs: health, education, housing, and a minimum control on goods. Regional planning can be the tool to integrate and coordinate the policies and the programs of the institution and can deal with housing, health, and education together with social welfare action at a regional level.

The social budget will be the register of all costs and transfers related to the above mentioned needs of the citizen or region. These costs, both capital or/and running costs, and transfers will reflect the decision-maker's ability to allocate the necessary funds (% of GDP; % of the budget) without jeopardizing productive investment requirements (% of GDP) to sustain economic growth. Regional planning will ensure the equitable allocation of resources within the regions of the kingdom. The main objective of such a budget is to improve the standard of living of the population, especially of the lowest household income bracket. Such an objective is based implicitly on a set of criteria regarding basic needs, the poverty line, and the imbalance in income distribution. A governing body sets out objectives and follows up achievement, and an information system secures continuous feedback between the governing body and citizens.

In these circumstances, the minimum pension becomes a tool of the redistribution policy, and payments for the social budget are accounted for as a major monetary aspect of the redistribution policy (securing minimum control on goods). The dynamic process of the extension of coverage of social security to all Jordanians will in time replace social welfare transfers as a means of improving distribution and will reduce such transfers to the lowest possible level. The social welfare action of the government and charitable societies will handle only cases of the disabled and families without financial resources and will give help only as a complement to the minimum pension in cases in which families have temporary financial difficulties.

3.2 Wage Policy

Redistribution is an attempt from outside the market to correct market forces regarding income distribution. Such a policy has a tendency to reconcile economic efficacy and social equity. The increasing action of pressure groups and continuous open social bargaining (dialogue) between social partners both push toward a readjustment of wages to match the increase in the cost of living and to share out the gains obtained by higher productivity.

The objective of such a policy is to maintain growth and stabilize prices. An operational criterion is production per capita, which accounts for gains in productivity and takes into consideration the number of hours of work per week and the proportion of unemployed in the active population. Nevertheless, the long-term effects of a wages policy will be to favor the increase of low wages and reduce wage differentials among workers of the same sector and/or of the same profile.

But a certain number of difficulties arise. Modern sectors of the economy where productivity is high will in time overtake all other sectors of the economy in terms of wage structure and profit-wage ratio, and any wage policy will soon become a de facto multilevel wage policy. This might have a negative effect on productivity and could reduce profit levels and investments. The experience of introducing a wages policy in some of the industrialized countries--for example, Great Britain, Sweden, and France in the 1970s--has shown the limits of such policies even where the labor market is well organized and there is government control of the public sector and major economic sectors.

If a comprehensive wage policy is difficult to implement, a minimum wage policy is more straightforward. A minimum wage for unskilled labor accepted by all social partners would introduce a regulatory tool in the labor market, ensuring for all a minimum command on goods compatible with basic needs in addition to other nonmonetary forms of remuneration and aid. This minimum wage would form the basis of future pensions and serve as an operational concept to the broad social policy in terms of wealth redistribution. It goes without saying that the existence of a minimum wage would contribute to the elaboration of a more viable actuarial review of the social insurance scheme, which would make more accurate financial planning possible.

The implementation of a minimum wage policy would face a certain number of practical problems and create a dynamic process of constant review of this minimum wage, perhaps also creating tensions between social partners, but the government could play the role of arbitrator. An approach combining redistribution (social budget of the nation) with a minimum wage policy merits further examination and discussion.

Notes

1. R.G. Hubbard and K.L. Judd: "Social Security and Individual Welfare." *American Economic Review 77* (September 1987), p. 630-643.

2. Department of Statistics: *Employment Survey, 1986* (Amman, n.d.), Table 20.

Bibliography

Department of Statistics: *Employment Survey, 1986.* Amman, n.d.
_____: *Statistical Yearbook, 1987.* Amman, n.d.
Fletcher, M.E.: *Economics and Social Problems.* Boston: Houghton Mifflin, 1979.
Hubbard, R.G., and Judd, K. L.: "Social Security and Individual Welfare." *American Economic Review 77* (September 1987).
International Social Security Association: *The Planning of Social Security.* Geneva: ISSA, 1971.
_____: *The Current Issues in Social Security Planning: Concepts and Techniques.* Geneva: ISSA, 1973.
_____: *Methods of Evaluating the Effectiveness of Social Security Programmes.* Geneva: ISSA 1976.
_____: *International Conference of Social Security Actuaries and Statisticians.* Mexico: ISSA 1979.
Mehmet, Ozay : *Economic Planning and Social Justice in Developing Countries.* London: Croom Helm, 1978.
Reynolds, Lloyd George: *Labour Economics and Labour Relations.* Englewood Cliffs, N.J.: Prentice-Hall, 1978.
Smadi, Mohammad, Ali, M.I.T., Amerah, M.S., and Ibrahim, I.J.: *The Unemployment Problem in Jordan: Characteristics and Prospects.* Amman: Royal Scientific Society, November 1987.

10

Health Care Expenditure and Its Impact on Income Groups

Abed Kharabsheh

1. Introduction

Health care expenditure in Jordan has increased in recent decades. During the period 1978-1986, the annual average increase was about JD 8 million. As a result, more resources have been devoted to the health care sector, an important development that should be studied and analyzed to help identify the main characteristics of this sector and reach some policy recommendations.

This chapter will focus on several aspects of health care in Jordan: the status of the health care system, the providers of health care, labor in the health care sector, the regional distribution of health care services, health care expenditure from 1970 to 1986, and the impact of health care expenditure on different income groups. In addition, some recommendations will be presented at the end of this chapter.

2. The Status of the Health Care System

The present health care system in Jordan is characterized by a maldistribution of health sector resources across the geographic areas and social groups of the kingdom. This maldistribution is reflected both in the volume and type of services offered. The health care system is very hospital oriented. Hospitals accounted for an estimated 75-80% of the Ministry of Health's budget during the period 1984-1988, while the share of primary health services was about 12.5%. The nonprimary health expenditure pattern of the nation (including the military medical services, the University Hospital, and the private sector) constitutes approximately 90% of the total expenditure on health care. Given the current health profile of Jordan, this large expenditure on hospitals is inefficient for several reasons. First, a great number of the cases dealt with by the hospitals could have initially been prevented or cared for below the hospital level. Second, given the location of the hospitals, only those people living in and around the major cities have health care available to them. For example, in the late 1970s, more than 80% of the country's physicians were based in Amman. This percentage had decreased to 63.2% by 1986. Most of the remainig physicians were based in the four other major urban centers: Zarqa, Irbid, Salt, and Karak. Third, hospitals are more capital intensive than other methods of health care provision, which leads to overutilization and increasing costs of health care and cost per patient day.[1] Fourth, in 1986, about 56.5% of all hospital beds were located in Amman, resulting in a bed/population ratio of 1:390.5 in the Amman governorate, compared with 1:533 for the country as a whole.[2]

Health care in Jordan is characterized by a relatively large spread of provider organizations operating to a significant degree independently of each other. The fragmented character of the delivery system is particularly noticeable as this is a country of only three million people, most of whom live in a relatively small area. The various providers of health care have been functioning largely in an uncoordinated manner, leading to duplication of efforts, an unequal spread of resources both geographically and between providers, and an inefficient use of these scarce health sector resources.

The three major public sector bodies providing health care are the Ministry of Health (MoH), the Royal Medical Services (RMS), and Jordan University Hospital (JUH). Other public sector health service activities are carried out through the Ministry of Education (school health), the Ministry of Labor and Social Affairs (health insurance schemes), and the Municipal Health Departments of Amman, Zarqa, and Irbid. Nongovernment providers include modern private practitioners, traditional midwives, the United Nations Relief and Works Agency (UNRWA), and various religious and charitable bodies.

In 1986, some of the main health indicators in Jordan were as follows:

- The infant mortality rate was about 0.06 (6 per 100 live births).
- Life expectancy at birth was sixty-seven years for males and seventy-one years for females.
- Facilities and services: 13.24 physicians per 10,000 inhabitants; 19 hospital beds per 10,000 inhabitants.

3. Providers of Health Care

Health care is mainly provided by the MoH, RMS, JUH, the private sector, and the UNRWA.

3.1 The Ministry of Health

In 1986, Ministry of Health institutions provided about 60% of health care in Jordan including approximately 37% of all hospital beds. The ministry is the only provider of preventive care. It is responsible for supervision of the private sector and the development of a national health policy. Despite a fee structure, its services are most often provided free of charge.

The MoH provides primary health care services through health centers; country clinics, which are health centers with a reduced level of services; mother and child health centers, which provide medical care and regular checkups for mothers and children; chest disease centers; and dental clinics. In 1986, the number of patients visiting these centers amounted to about 7 million.

In addition, the MoH provides the school health and environmental health services. It is responsible for the analysis of drinking water, the food hygiene inspectorate, and health education services.

In 1986, the MoH reportedly had 197 health centers, 227 country clinics, 102 mother and child health care centers, 58 dental clinics, and 15 hospitals with 1,988 beds, or 37.3% of the total number of hospital beds in Jordan. The occupancy rate was 71.34%, and the average length of stay was four days.[3]

3.2 Royal Medical Services

The RMS provides care to active military and security personnel and their dependents. In 1986, the RMS provided health services to about 630,000 individuals, or 31.4% of the population. These services provided all types of care. In 1982, the RMS had fourteen centers giving primary care and six hospitals.[4]

In 1986, the RMS had 1,358 beds, or 25.9% of the country's hospital beds. The occupancy rate was 76.3%, and the average stay was 5.8 days.

3.3 Jordan University Hospital

This hospital is a comprehensive medical hospital as well as a teaching center. It provides care to university employees, patients insured by the MoH, and private patients. According to annual statistics, in 1985 about 91,545 outpatients visited hospital departments, 37,155 patients came to the hospital as emergency cases, and 20,155 patients were admitted. In 1986, the occupancy rate of the hospital was 75%, and the average length of stay was six days.

In terms of physicians, the hospital's participation in the provision of medical care accounted for about 5% of the total health care services. In 1986, there were 481 beds which was 9.1% of the total number of hospital beds in Jordan.

3.4 UNRWA

UNRWA health services are available only to refugees registered with UNRWA and to people who work with UNRWA. Data related to health care provided by UNRWA are listed in Table 10.1. According to the data, UNRWA provides health care for outpatients in seventeen health centers. It provides inpatient care (hospital services) in two private hospitals, where a total of thirty-eight beds are funded. Curative and preventive dental care services are provided by twelve permanent centers and one mobile dental team for the Jordan Valley. Laboratory services, radiology facilities, and so on are also provided.

3.5 The Private Sector

In 1986, the private sector provided secondary health care through twenty-eight hospitals with a total of 1,535 beds and a number of private clinics distributed in all cities. The number of physicians in the private sector constitutes 41.9% of the total number of physicians in Jordan. The majority of these worked in big cities. In 1986, the private sector was responsible for:[5]

- 53.9% of the total number of hospitals in Jordan
- 27.6% of the total number of hospital beds
- The majority of hospitals in Amman (about 80%)
- Average patient stay: two to three days
- Occupancy rate: 55%
- Number of physicians: 1,550
- Number of dentists: 400

TABLE 10.1
UNRWA Health Care Services, 1986

Health Care Data	In Camps	Outside Camps	Total
Health centers/points	10	7	17
Daily average number of medical consultations	2,500	376	2,876
Dental treatment: cases per year			53,740
Number of subsidized beds			38
Total registered refugees (1987)			852,746
UNRWA staff in Jordan			5,384
Health budget in JD [a]			1,150,000
UNWRA percentage share of total health expenditure [b]			1

[a] The health budget amounts to 18% of the total UNRWA budget in Jordan.
[b] In Jordan, 1986.

Source: UNRWA publications, January 1987, Amman.

- Number of pharmacists: 1,100
- Number of staff nurses: 372
- Number of midwives: 93
- Number of health technicians: 427

4. Health Care Sector Personnel

Health care personnel consists of physicians, nurses, trained midwives, practical or assistant nurses, nurses under training, dentists, and other categories of personnel such as pharmacists and medical technicians. Table 10.2 gives a clear outline of labor distribution in the health care sector:

It is clear from Table 10.2 that the participation of the public sector in health care provision for the nation in terms of physicians is 58%, while for the private sector it is 42%; the participation in terms of dentists is 35.4%, while for the private sector it is 64.6%. The participation of the public sector in terms of pharmacists is 11%, while for the private sector it is 89%. Public participation in terms of nurses is 77%, while for the private sector it is 22.9%. Public participation in terms of midwives is 71.7%, while for the private sector it is 28.3%.

The development of labor power in health care for 1978-1986 can be seen in Tables 10.3 and 10.4.

When we compare the number of physicians in 1986 with the number for 1978, we see that the number of physicians more than doubled in both the public and the private sectors. The same can also be said for numbers of dentists, pharmacists and nurses. This phenomenon underlines the fact that more resources were directed at the health care sector. Despite a rapid increase in Jordanian health care personnel, there is still a serious

TABLE 10.2
Health Care Personnel, 1986

Personnel	MOH	JUH	RMS	Total Public Sector	Private Sector	Total	Average per 10,000 population
Physicians	1,240	189	724	2,153	1,550	3,703	13.24
Dentists	99	1	119	219	400	619	2.20
Pharmacists	89	5	42	136	1,100	1,236	4.40
Nurses	394	288	573	1,255	372	1,627	5.80
Midwives [a]	208	4	24	236	93	329	30.00

[a] Average is per 10,000 living children.

Source : Ministry of Health, Department of Planning, *Statistical Annual Report, 1986* (Amman, n.d.).

TABLE 10.3
Distribution of Physicians by Provider, 1978-1986

Provider	1978	1979	1980	1981	1982	1983	1984	1985	1986
MOH	469	588	629	675	735	778	934	1,110	1,240
JUH	89	119	138	147	153	160	170	177	189
RMS	356	416	460	451	474	510	597	643	724
Private sector	580	800	948	1,144	1,300	983	1,208	1,289	1,550
Total	1,494	1,893	2,175	2,417	2,662	2,431	2,909	3,219	3,703
Physician-index [a]	7.20	8.90	9.80	10.50	11.10	11.00	11.20	12.00	13.24

[a] Number of physicians per 10,000 of population.

Source: Ministry of Health, Department of Planning, *Statistical Annual Report, 1985 and 1986* (Amman, n.d.).

shortage of nurses of Jordanian nationality. Jordan currently imports about 35% of its need for nursing services from outside--mainly from Pakistan, India, and the Phillippines. But at the end of 1988, 835 nurses under training in universities and colleges were expected to graduate. This will reduce the dependency on nursing services from outside Jordan. In 1986, the numbers of allied medical groups in different areas and with respect to different health care providers were as shown in Table 10.5.

5. Regional Distribution of Health Care Services

In 1986, there were fifty-two hospitals in Jordan, twenty-eight of them belonging to the private sector, fifteen to the MoH, eight to the RMS, and last but not least Jordan University Hospital. The distribution of beds

TABLE 10.4
Development of Labor Groups, [a] 1978-1986.

	1978	1979	1980	1981	1982	1983	1984	1985	1986
Physicians	1,494	1,893	2,175	2,417	2,662	2,431	2,909	3,219	3,703
Dentists	302	323	393	500	523	545	566	539	619
Pharmacists	417	515	572	678	677	867	745	972	1,236
Nurses	762	803	904	916	1.205	1,236	1,370	1,441	1,627
Midwives	208	227	230	238	272	330	314	291	329

[a] Absolute numbers.

Source: Ministry of Health, Department of Planning, *Statistical Annual Report, 1986* (Amman, n.d.).

TABLE 10.5
Distribution of Health Technicians According to Specialization and Provider, 1986

	Provider					
Specialization	MOH	RMS	JUH	UNWRA	Private Sector	Total
Lab-technician	292	195	59	12	383	941
X-ray technician	115	92	28	-	47	282
Pharmacist assistant	303	123	24	22	289	761
Anethesist technician	114	40	59	-	15	228
Physiotherapy technician	42	56	6	-	-	104
Dentist technician	62	82	-	-	18	162
Statistics and medical record technician	123	-	53	16	58	250
Health inspector	187	23	-	30	-	241
Nurse assistant	642	1,817	280	85	427	3,201

Source: Ministry of Health, Department of Planning, *Statistical Annual Report, 1986* (Amman, n.d.), p. 51.

according to cities is shown in Table 10.6.

The public sector is the major supplier of hospital beds. In 1986, more than one-half of all hospital beds in Jordan were concentrated in Amman (56.5%). The average number of beds per 10,000 of the population was 18.8 beds.

More specifically, the number of beds ranged from as high as 28.9 per 10,000 population in Mafraq to as low as 8.7 in Tafileh. Amman, with 25.6 beds per 10,000 population, was well above the national average. In contrast, the figures for Zarqa, Karak, Ma'an, and Aqaba were below average. Since Mafraq is the smallest governorate by population (see Table 10.7), it might be treated as an exceptional case. We are then left with the result that in 1986, Amman showed a significantly better beds/population ratio than did other areas of Jordan.

Not surprisingly, Amman had the highest percentage share of Jordan's total capacity of hospital beds. Next came Irbid and Zarqa, which together accounted for about three out of ten beds in Jordan. According to Table 10.6, not more than 15.3% of the total number of beds were to be found in the remaining governorates.

The participation of the public sector in the provision of hospital beds was essential in all governorates, ranging from 62.1% in Zarqa to 100% in Balqa, Tafileh, Ma'an, and Aqaba. Public hospitals played a positive role in decreasing the regional inequality in this respect. Without public sector engagement, there would have been no beds in the cities and areas of Ma'an, Aqaba, Tafileh, and Balqa. Nevertheless, the number of beds per 10,000 population was still low in these governorates. The bulk of public

TABLE 10.6
Distribution of Hospital Beds, 1986

Location	Public Sector Providers [a]	Private Sector Providers	Total	Share (%)	Beds per 10,000 population
Amman	1,979	983	2,962	56.5	25.6
Zarqa	440	269	709	13.5	17.5
Balqa	333	-	333	6.3	17.1
Irbid	645	128	773	14.7	11.3
Mafraq	73	40	113	2.2	28.9
Karak	134	30	164	3.1	13.1
Tafileh	36	-	36	0.7	8.7
Ma'an and Aqaba	156	-	156	3.0	15.9
Total	3,796	1,450	5,246	100.0	18.8

[a] Public sector consists of MoH, JUH, and RMS.

Source: Ministry of Health, Department of Planning, *Statistical Annual Report, 1986* (Amman, n.d.), p.34.

hospital beds came from the Ministry of Health. In 1986, the public provision of hospital beds throughout Jordan amounted to 3,796.

In 1986, the MoH had the highest number of beds (1,958), and its proportion of the total number of beds was 37.3%. The second highest number was provided by the RMS, with 25.9%. Finally, JUH provided 9.2% of the total, or 481 out of 5,246 beds.

Another important indicator of regional health care provision is the number of physicians available. As will be discussed, the capital city of Amman again showed a high concentration, while Mafraq was an exceptional case, albeit in the opposite direction to the aforementioned findings on provision of beds.

The distribution of physicians according to governorates is shown in Table 10.7.

According to the final column of Table 10.7, in 1986, 63% of the physicians were in Amman governorate, resulting in this governorate having the highest number of physicians per 10,000 of population (20.0). The other governorates had from 8 to 9.5, except Mafraq, which had only 6 physicians per 10,000. The high concentration of physicians in Amman brought the national average to 13.2 physicians per 10,000 of population. In other words, 1 physician was available for every 755 inhabitants (Jordanian nationals). This average varied considerably, from 494 per physicain in Amman to more than 1,000 in all other areas of Jordan. The highest number of people per physician was in Mafraq, where it reached 1,595.

A third indicator of practical relevance is the regional distribtuion of

TABLE 10.7
Distribution of Physicians According to Governorates, 1986

Governorate	Population	Physicians	Physicians/10,000 of Population	Physicians/ Population	Share (%)
Amman	1,156,903	2,340	20.2	1: 494	63.2
Zarqa	404,457	355	9.0	1:1,139	9.6
Balqa	194,345	152	8.0	1:1,279	4.1
Irbid	681,654	552	8.0	1:1,235	14.9
Mafraq	94,098	59	6.0	1:1,595	1.6
Karak	125,512	115	9.5	1:1,091	3.1
Tafileh	41,520	37	9.0	1:1,122	1.0
Ma'an and Aqaba	97,572	93	9.5	1:1,049	2.5
Total	2,796,061	3,703	13.2	1: 755	100.0

Source : Ministry of Health, Department of Planning, *Statistical Annual Report, 1986* (Amman, n.d.), Table 25, p.47.

primary health care services in Jordan. In 1986, the MoH reported on four kinds of service: primary health centers, village clinics, mother and child health clinics, and dental clinics. Although the report included the governorate of Amman, few or no primary health care services will be located in the urban center.

Table 10.8 demonstrates that Irbid had the highest number of primary health centers, village clinics, mother and child health clinics, and dental clinics, followed by Amman and Karak. The lowest ranking governorate in this respect was Tafileh. Tafileh showed the lowest number of primary

TABLE 10.8
Distribution of Primary Health Services, 1986

Governorate	Primary Health Centers	Village Clinics	Mother and Child Health Centers	Dental Clinics
Amman/Madaba	27	37	17	15
Zarqa	15	14	14	6
Balqa	26	17	11	5
Irbid	66	41	34	18
Mafraq	18	32	4	4
Karak	18	38	16	4
Tafileh	7	8	3	2
Ma'an and Aqaba	12	35	3	4
Total	197	227	102	58

Source : Ministry of Health, Department of Planning, *Statistical Annual Report, 1986* (Amman, n.d.), pp. 146-149.

health care establishments in all four categories. Ma'an and Aqaba also shared a small proportion of such services: 6.1% of all primary health care centers, 15.4% of all village clinics, 2.9% of the total of mother and child health clinics, and 6.9% of the dental clinics. Because the numbers in Table 10.8 have to be considered in relation to population size and the rural/urban structure of areas, any conclusions we may draw will not be straightforward. Nevertheless, primary health services in Jordan my ease some of the earlier mentioned imbalances in regional distribution of health care services.

6. Health Care Expenditure from 1978 to 1986

According to the final column of Table 10A.1 the percentage ratio of total health care expenditure to gross national product (GNP) ranged from about 4% in 1981 to 5.5% in 1986. The ratio has risen steadily since 1981 but fluctuated before that. It can be seen from Table 10.9 that the private sector is an important source of health care. Its share of the total annual health care expenditure ranged from 45% in 1981 to 39% in 1986. The MoH share of expenditure ranged from 33% in 1979 to 27% in 1981. The RMS share of expenditure ranged from about 15% in 1979 to 20% in 1984. JUH occupied fourth place with ratios of expenditure ranged from about 7% in 1978 to 10% in 1986. UNRWA ratios ranged from about 2% in 1978 to about 1% in 1986.

The participation of the public sector ranged from about 54% (of the total health expenditure) in 1981 to 60% in 1986, while the private sector and UNRWA accounted for the remaining percentages. Per capita health care expenditure increased gradually throughout the whole period (see Table 10A.1) from JD 17.080 per annum in 1978 to JD 37.550 in 1986.

TABLE 10.9
Providers' Share of Health Care Expenditure, 1978-1986 (%)

Year	MOH	JUH	RMS	Private Sector	UNRWA	Total
1978	29.3	6.6	18.5	43.6	2.1	100.0
1979	32.9	9.0	15.1	41.7	1.8	100.0
1980	29.9	8.9	19.2	40.0	1.9	100.0
1981	27.4	8.4	18.6	44.7	1.9	100.0
1982	31.1	7.1	18.2	41.9	1.4	100.0
1983	29.9	7.0	19.2	42.4	1.5	100.0
1984	27.4	9.3	19.6	42.2	1.5	100.0
1985	31.1	9.3	18.9	39.3	1.4	100.0
1986	32.1	9.8	18.2	39.0	1.2	100.0

Source: Calculated from Table 10A.1.

The average annual growth of expenditure during the period 1978-1986 was as follows:[6] JD 3.15 million in the private sector, JD 2.09 million in the MoH, JD 1.65 million in the RMS, and JD 8.36 million in the health sector as a whole.

7. Impact of Health Expenditure on Different Income Groups

To find the impact of health care expenditure on different income groups, we can study health care expenditure as a special item of the family expenditure survey carried out by the Department of Statistics in 1986.

Using data from this survey, we can see that in 1986 average annual per capita health care expenditure in Jordan was JD 9.400. The percentage share of health care expenditure in relation to expenditure on all groups of commodities and services was reported to be 1.8%. It should be kept in mind that the survey covered personal spending of private households. Thus, the health care expenditure figures did not reflect the true cost of health care in Jordan per household or individual. In 1986, no attempt was undertaken to calculate the total per capita health care expenditure in Jordan. It was certainly considerably higher than the aforementioned private per capita expenditure. In fact, public sector per capita expenditure was as high as JD 37.500. Nevertheless, the analysis that follows is confined to the findings of the 1986 survey.

According to the first column of Table 10.10, average annual per capita health care expenditure in urban areas (JD 11.300) was higher than in rural areas (JD 5.500). With respect to individual governorates, Amman governorate represented the highest per capita expenditure (JD 13.800), followed by Balqa governorate (JD 8.500). The lowest per capita expenditure was in Ma'an governorate (JD 1.900). There was a tremendous difference in per capita expenditure--sevenfold in Amman as compared to Ma'an. Southern regions of Karak, Tafileh, and Ma'an spent significantly lower amounts than did the northern regions of Irbid, Mafraq, Balqa, and Zarqa.

At this point, it is interesting to relate the revealed private health care demand as stated in Table 10.10 with the health care supply enumerated in Tables 10.6 to 10.8. Obviously, the highest level of both supply and demand was found in Amman governorate. It might tentatively be concluded that the greatest ability to pay was in the capital city and that this created a correspondingly high supply level, especially with respect to the private sector (Table 10.6). Next in actual demand came Balqa governorate, which, surprisingly, had no private supply of hospital beds (Table 10.6), one of the lowest ratios of physicians per 10,000 population (Table 10.7), and an average share of primary health services

TABLE 10.10
Average Per Capita Health Care Expenditure as Percentage of Total Household Expenditure, 1986.

Location	Per Capita Health Care Expenditure (JD)	Health Care Expenditure as % of total Household Expenditure
Amman	13.800	2.0
Irbid and Mafraq	6.200	1.6
Balqa	8.500	2.1
Karak and Tafileh	4.200	1.2
Zarqa	7.200	1.4
Ma'an	1.900	0.6
Urban	11.300	1.9
Rural	5.500	1.4
Jordan	9.400	1.8

Source: Department of Statistics, Household Expenditure and Income Survey, 1986 (Amman, n.d.), Table 0801.

(Table 10.8). Such a discrepancy can only partly be explained by geographical location; Balqa is adjacent to Amman governorate and most of its population can easily reach Amman hospitals.

With respect to reported annual health care expenditure, one interesting feature is the level and percentage of spending as a function of size of household. According to Table 10.11, the size of the household affects the level of per capita health care expenditure. If the size of the household was either one, two, or three individuals, health care expenditure per capita was greater than JD 20, whereas in households with at least ten members, health care expenditure per capita was no more than JD 6. Households with fewer than eight individuals spent more on health care per capita than the average of the kingdom (JD 9.400); those households with at least eight individuals spent less than the per capita average for the kingdom. The ratio of medical care expenditure to total expenditure ranged from 2.7% in the smallest household group (one individual) to 1.4% for households with ten to eleven individuals.

Table 10.12 indicates that personal health care expenditure depends on the level of education. Per capita health care expenditure correlated positively with the level of education of the head of the household. Those educated to postgraduate level showed the highest expenditure per capita (JD 26.100), whereas those who were illiterate spent the least (JD 6.900). In families in which the head of the household was educated to secondary level or beyond, per capita expenditure was higher than JD 9.400; when the head of household was not educated to secondary level, per capita expen-

TABLE 10.11
Average Per Capita Health Care Expenditure According to Household Size, 1986

Household Size	Per Capita Health Care Expenditure (JD)	Health Care Expenditure as % of Total Household Expenditure
1	22.500	2.7
2-3	27.400	2.6
4-5	17.800	2.2
6-7	10.100	1.7
8-9	6.800	1.5
10-11	5.900	1.4
12+	6.000	1.7
Average	9.400	1.8

Source: Department of Statistics, *Household Expenditure and Income Survey, 1986* (Amman, n.d.), Table 0802.

diture was less than JD 9.400.

These rankings may take a somewhat different order when expenditure shares are considered. In this case, the level of personal income shows its influence on the level of personal health care expenditure. Because, on average, the higher educated earn higher incomes, their ability to pay for health services is higher. Accordingly, a high amount of expenditure in absolute terms, or JD, does not necessarily lead to an equally high percentage share of health care expenditure by the well educated. The last column of Table 10.12 indicates the following: The least well educated (illiterate; reads and writes) and holders of a bachelor's degree spent close to the national average of 1.8%. Significantly less than 1.8% was spent by heads of household with preparatory and elementary school education. Holders of intermediate college degrees and those holding of master and Ph.D. gedrees spent a great deal more than the national average. Remarkably, a household with head of household carrying a bachelor's degree showed both a higher average total expenditure and lower JD per capita health care spending than did those with an intermediate college degree.

Health care expenditure per capita is affected by the employment status of the head of the household. Where the head of the household is either an unpaid worker or a domestic worker, he or she does not pay anything for medical care; for other categories of employment status there is positive health care expenditure per capita. In 1986, the highest level of expenditure was associated with the employer category (JD 17.100), followed by the self-employed (JD 10.900), and then wage earners (JD 7.900). Data on employment status and health care expendi-

TABLE 10.12

Average Per Capita Health Care Expenditure by Education and as Expenditure Share in All Groups of Commodities and Services, 1986

Head of Household Level of Education	Per Capita Health Care Expenditure (JD)	Health Care Expenditure as % of Commodities and Services Expenditure
Master's degree and Ph.D.	26.100	2.8
Bachelor's degree	15.400	1.7
Intermediate college	18.600	2.6
Secondary	13.700	2.0
Preparatory	8.000	1.5
Elementary	7.900	1.5
Reads and Write	8.400	1.9
Illiterate	6.900	1.7
Average	9.400	1.8

Source: Department of Statistics, *Household Expenditure and Income Survey, 1986* (Amman, n.d.), Table 0806.

ture can be found in Table 0810 of the Household Expenditure and Income Survey. According to that table, employers and self-employed spent around 2% of total expenditure on health care, compared with 1.6% spent by wage earners. Apparently, any health care that was provided for households whose head of household was either an unpaid or a household worker was free of charge. Whether this means redistribution of health care in favor of the needy, deserves further investigation.

Average annual health care expenditure per capita is also affected by the type of economic activity the head of the household is involved in. In 1986, as is indicated in Table 10.13, the highest annual expenditure per capita was in trade and restaurants (JD 14.900), followed by finance and banking (JD 13.200), construction (JD 11.800), and electricity, gas, and water (JD 10.400). These types of households spent more than the national average. Less than national average JD per capita health care expenditure was found in agriculture (JD 5.400), transportation (JD 7.200), mining and quarrying (JD 7.700), other services (JD 7.900), and industry (JD 8.700).

Comparison with Table 5A.2 (Chapter 5), which gives average wage levels for economic activities, reveals a positive correlation between health care spending and wage level. But this relationship does not hold for transportation and tourism. More specifically, transportation ranks second from the top level of wages and ranks second from the bottom in the level of JD per capita health care spending. This discrepancy cannot be fully explained by the differences in the two samples, particularly a deviation between levels of expenditure, income, and wage. It is also interesting to note that the ranking with respect to health expenditure share of total expenditure was by and large preserved. Again, trade came first and agriculture last. The exceptional case was finance and banking, which was the top level economic activity with respect to wages. According to Table 10.13, its health care expenditure share was less than the national average. There is no straightforward explanation for this phenomenon. Health care expenditure per capita in households involved in all other economic activities was less than the annual average (per capita) expenditure for the kingdom (JD 9.400).

Finally, as shown in Table 10.14, the average annual health care expenditure per capita is also affected by the level of total annual household expenditure. The highest health care expenditure per capita, JD 20.600, was associated with the group with the highest annual expenditure, but the highest proportion of health care expenditure per capita in total expenditure on all groups of commodities and services, 5.5%, was associated with the group with the lowest total annual expenditure level (less than JD 600 per annum). By and large, the JD per capita health care expenditure increased with the level of total annual household expenditure from JD 1,200 upward. A strikingly different relationship was reported for the low expenditure groups of less than JD 1,200 annually. They spent a fairly high amount on health care not only in relative but also in absolute

TABLE 10.13
Average Per Capita Health Care Expenditure by Economic Activity and as a Share in All Groups of Commodities and Services, 1986

Head of Household Economic Activity	Per Capita Health Care Expenditure (JD)	Health Care Expenditure as % of Commodities and Services Expenditure
Agriculture	5.400	1.2
Mining and quarrying	7.700	1.2
Industry	8.700	1.6
Electricity, gas, and water	10.400	2.1
Construction	11.800	2.4
Trade and restaurants	14.900	2.5
Transportation	7.200	1.6
Finance and banking	13.200	1.5
Other services	7.900	1.6
Average [a]	9.000	1.7

[a] Average can diviate from those in previous tables due to decrease of sample size (unspecified economic activities).

Source: Department of Statistics, *Household Expenditure and Income Survey, 1986* (Amman, n.d.), Table 0811.

TABLE 10.14

Average Per Capita Health Care Expenditure by Household Expenditure and as Expenditure Share in All Groups of Commodities and Services, 1986

Annual Household Expenditure	Per Capita Health Care Expenditure (JD)	Health Care Expenditure as % of Commodities and Services Expenditure
less than 600	16.800	5.5
600-1,199	5.200	2.3
1,200-1,799	3.000	1.3
1,800-2,399	5.300	1.8
2,400-2,999	6.500	1.8
3,000-3,599	6.500	1.5
3,600-4,199	11.000	2.2
4,200-4,799	10.200	1.6
4,800-5,399	10.900	1.8
5,400-5,999	12.300	2.0
6,000-6,599	15.300	2.0
6,600-7,199	13.600	1.5
7,200+	20.600	1.7
Average [a]	9.200	1.8

[a] Average can deviate from previous tables due to decrease in sample size.

Source: Department of Statistics, *Household Expenditure and Income Survey, 1986* (Amman, n.d.), Table 0812.

terms. More light needs to be shed on the somewhat strange observation that the lowest total expenditure groups (less than JD 600 annually) came second in JD per capita health care expenditure, outranked only by the highest total expenditure groups (more than JD 7,200 annually). The group with the lowest total expenditure was thus placed well above the average per capita health care expenditure in Jordan. In addition to the lowest group, groups with an annual expenditure in excess of JD 3,600 had health care expenditure per capita higher than the annual average for the kingdom (JD 9.400), whereas expenditure per capita of the other expenditure groups was below this average.

8. Conclusions and Recommendations

There is a shortage of information about the health care sector in Jordan. Data are fragmented, and statistics are not readily available. To solve the problem, the department of planning of the MoH has to find new ways of collecting socioeconomic data affecting health care. The various providers of health care should cooperate in order to provide the department of planning with all necessary data related to the health care sector. This approach will help researchers in health care economics to find what they need in their field of study.

The findings of this chapter and the recommendations can be summarized as follows:

1. Health care in Jordan is found to be hospital oriented. Hospitals are capital intensive-institutions. This leads to an increased average cost of each unit of health care produced, especially when the low occupancy rate in hospitals is taken into account, which may also increase the cost of a patient's day in hospital. To solve this problem, it is necessary to concentrate more on primary and secondary health care through the establishment of primary and comprehensive health care centers. This policy has recently been adopted by the Ministry of Health.

2. There is a heavy concentration of hospitals, hospital beds, and physicians in the Amman governorate and, to a lesser extent, in the other main cities. To counter this development, it is necessary to redistribute health care services by providing incentives that would encourage physicians to take jobs in rural areas rather than cities and help private physicians to establish private clinics in rural areas.

3. The ability to pay for health care services is not the same for all people. It differs according to the type of insurance, the institution or sector an individual works for, and level of income. To align the ability to pay with the individual's need for health care, more coordination in the health care sector is required to establish an appropriate comprehensive insurance plan. Such a plan should make health care services available to those who need these services regardless of their ability to pay.

4. Research into the health care sector has been very limited in Jordan thus far. More efforts are required to establish what the main problems of this sector are and to suggest appropriate solutions.

Notes

1. Steven R. Eastaugh: *Medical Economics and Health Finance* (Boston: Auburn House, 1981); National Medical Enterprises, *Jordan Country and Health Profile* (Amman: NME International, n.d.).

2. In 1986, the number of hospital beds in Amman was 2,952 and in Jordan, 5,246; the number of people in Amman was 1,156,903 and in the whole country 2,796,061.

3. Ministry of Health, Department of Planning, *Statistical Annual Report, 1986* (Amman, n.d.), p.98.

4. Ministry of Health, Department of Planning, *Statistical Annual Report, 1982* (Amman, n.d.).

5. Ministry of Health, Department of Planning, *Statistical Annual Report, 1986* (Amman, n.d.).

6. The annual growth was found by using a simple linear model of each provider's expenditure as a dependent variable and time as an independent variable.

Bibliography

Central Bank of Jordan: *Monthly Statistical Bulletin 24.* Amman, April 1988.

Department of Statistics: *Household Expenditure and Income Survey, 1986.* Amman, n.d.

Eastaugh, S.R.: *Medical Economics and Health Finance.* Boston: Auburn House, 1981.

Feldstein, J.P.: *Health Care Economics.* New York: Wiley, 1983.

Ministry of Health, Department of Planning: *Statistical Annual Reports, 1982, 1985, 1986.* Amman, various years.

National Medical Enterprises: *Jordan Country and Health Profile.* NME International, n.d.

United Nations Relief and Work Agency for Palestine Refugees in the Near East, Department of Information: *UNRWA Publication.* Amman: UNRWA, January 1987.

Appendix A

Statistical Appendix

TABLE 5A.1
Frequency Distribution of Workers [a] Covered by Social Security According to Wage Group and Major Economic Activity, Second Quarter 1987

Major Economic Activity	Wage Groups (JD)											Total
	<50	50-	100-	150-	200-	250-	300-	350-	400-	450-	500+	
Agriculture, fisheries, and forestry	287	12,696	1,200	236	79	44	16	17	20	13	61	14,669
Industry, mining, and energy	9,421	41,086	13,488	5,458	2,446	1,075	589	310	199	196	577	74,845
Wholesale and retail	2,913	13,644	4,414	1,811	697	436	245	159	98	98	235	24,750
Construction and building	1,241	29,046	16,416	5,768	1,973	891	588	330	145	160	697	57,255
Transport, storage, and communications	584	9,109	8,814	1,966	755	384	151	100	95	51	301	22,310
Finance and insurance services	169	5,225	5,420	1,602	667	367	256	206	115	103	377	14,507
Tourism	2,045	9,154	1,484	616	210	166	64	58	49	32	123	14,001
Other services	10,690	60,037	16,144	5,351	2,325	1,245	780	588	406	406	1075	99,047
Unclassified	3,333	54,887	12,430	2,872	1,689	663	309	241	104	106	440	77,074
Total	30,683	234,884	79,810	25,680	10,841	5,271	2,998	2,009	1,231	1,165	3,886	398,458

[a] Total number.

Source: Social Security Corporation, computer section.

TABLE 5A.2
Percentage Distribution of Workers [a] Covered by Social Security According to Wage Group and Main Profession, Second Quarter 1987

Main Profession	<50	50-	100-	150-	200-	250-	300-	350-	400-	450-	500+	Total %
Professionals and technicians	4.18	45.69	29.11	8.07	3.86	2.18	1.86	1.42	0.95	0.87	1.80	100.00
Managers, administrative workers	1.14	8.15	8.63	9.68	10.01	9.78	7.39	7.77	5.34	5.82	26.22	100.00
Clerical staff	1.97	54.45	26.60	8.71	3.59	1.81	1.03	0.63	0.28	0.25	0.68	100.00
Salespersons	3.39	51.48	23.86	9.32	4.08	2.57	1.23	1.23	0.63	0.73	1.48	100.00
Workers in services	15.08	75.85	6.78	1.30	0.35	0.17	0.08	0.05	0.05	0.04	0.24	100.00
Workers in agriculture	6.70	86.27	5.46	1.00	0.19	0.09	0.01	0.03	0.01	0.02	0.20	100.00
Production and transport workers	7.97	58.49	23.11	6.70	2.10	0.71	0.33	0.17	0.07	0.05	0.30	100.00
Unclassified	5.85	39.65	20.92	11.54	7.70	4.42	2.39	1.59	1.12	1.12	3.67	100.00

Wage Groups (JD)

[a] Total number.

Source: Social Security Corporation, computer section.

TABLE 5A.3
Percentage Distribution of Workers [a] Covered by Social Security According to Wage Group and Sex, Second Quarter 1987

| | | | | | Wage Groups (JD) | | | | | | |
Sex	<50	50-	100-	150-	200-	250-	300-	350-	400-	450-	500+	Total %
Male	6.97	58.76	20.47	6.55	2.80	1.38	0.80	0.54	0.33	0.32	1.07	100.00
Female	12.88	60.14	17.02	5.75	2.13	0.90	0.40	0.27	0.13	0.12	0.27	100.00
Unclassified	16.18	64.59	11.65	4.19	1.64	0.68	0.34	0.23	0.11	0.00	0.40	100.00

[a] Total number.

Source: Social Security Corporation, computer section.

TABLE 5A.4
Frequency Distribution of Workers [a] Covered by Social Security According to Wage Group and Governorate, Second Quarter 1987

Governorate	Wage Groups (JD)											Total
	<50	50-	100-	150-	200-	250-	300-	350-	400-	450-	500+	
Amman	24,677	162,137	59,190	19,539	8,024	4,241	2,146	1,565	1,018	945	3,229	286,711
Jerusalem	11	799	170	27	36	8	4	5	5	3	3	1,071
Irbid	2,904	21,066	5'447	1,445	623	230	315	179	80	104	209	32,602
Nablus	43	751	110	27	19	8	5	2	0	0	3	968
Hebron	1	331	34	5	6	1	0	0	0	0	2	380
Balqa	716	11,087	2,045	644	246	105	50	37	15	10	77	15,032
Karak	444	10,742	4,714	1,631	865	272	235	93	50	53	126	19,225
Ma'an	1,757	27,745	8,009	2,337	1,010	401	241	127	63	48	233	41,971
Unclassified	130	226	91	25	12	5	2	1	0	2	4	498
Total	30,683	234,884	27,810	25,680	10,841	5,271	2,998	2,009	1,231	1,165	3,886	398,458

[a] Total number.

Source: Social Security Corporation, computer section.

TABLE 5A.5
Frequency Distribution of Workers [a] Covered by Social Security According to Wage Group and Region, Second Quarter 1987

Region	Wage Groups (JD)											Total
	<50	50-	100-	150-	200-	250-	300-	350-	400-	450-	500+	
Jordan	13,731	149,934	57,864	19,671	8,600	4,181	2,278	1,579	952	890	2,500	262,180
Arab countries	14,436	65,328	10,758	1,945	754	277	147	105	79	83	386	94,298
African (non-Arab) countries	68	238	72	13	4	4	2	2	1	2	3	409
Asian (non-Arab) countries	1,148	9,276	7,303	2,672	789	368	230	120	72	59	193	22,230
Australia	0	0	3	1	3	9	1	2	2	0	3	24
Europe	31	581	307	192	171	190	162	106	77	88	582	2,487
Americas	9	61	64	61	60	33	29	27	12	15	69	440
Unclassified	1,260	9,466	3,439	1,125	460	209	149	68	36	28	150	16,390
Total	30,683	234,844	79,810	25,680	10,841	5,271	2,998	2,009	1,231	1,165	3,886	398,458

[a] Total numbers.

Source: Social Security Corporation, computer section.

TABLE 5A.6
Percentage Distribution of Jordanian Workers Covered by Social Security According to Wage Group and Major Activity, Second Quarter 1987

Major Economic Activity	Wage Groups (JD)											
	<50	50-	100-	150-	200-	250-	300-	350-	400-	450-	500+	Total %
Agriculture, fisheries, and forestry	1.29	87.39	7.96	1.63	0.54	0.35	0.12	0.12	0.13	0.07	0.37	100.00
Industry, mining, and energy	10.78	50.28	21.43	8.95	3.99	1.69	0.92	0.51	0.33	0.33	0.81	100.00
Wholesale and retail	11.69	49.79	20.45	8.67	3.41	2.16	1.18	0.81	0.46	0.47	0.92	100.00
Construction and building	1.55	42.75	31.38	12.83	4.95	2.40	1.20	0.83	0.41	0.43	1.26	100.00
Transport, storage, and communications	1.89	35.73	40.41	11.43	3.91	2.37	0.89	0.63	0.62	0.31	1.80	100.00
Finance and insurance services	1.11	35.32	38.12	11.16	4.65	2.57	1.77	1.44	0.81	0.71	2.33	100.00
Tourism	10.70	67.25	13.13	5.14	1.57	0.86	0.44	0.33	0.18	0.13	0.28	100.00
Other services	4.92	60.73	20.00	6.43	2.84	1.51	0.94	0.69	0.44	0.45	1.03	100.00
Unclassified	2.26	71.39	16.83	4.28	2.69	0.98	0.47	0.33	0.14	0.12	0.52	100.00

Source: Social Security Corporation, computer section.

TABLE 5A.7
Percentage Distribution of Non–Jordanian Workers Covered by Social Security According to Wage Group and Major Economic Activity, Second Quarter 1987

Major Economic Activity	Wage Groups (JD)												
	<50	50-	100-	150-	200-	250-	300-	350-	400-	450-	500+	Total %
Agriculture, fisheries, and forestry	5.12	82.52	9.21	1.50	0.51	0.08	0.04	0.08	0.16	0.16	0.63	100.00
Industry, mining, and energy	16.15	63.99	11.30	4.03	1.85	0.94	0.53	0.23	0.15	0.13	0.69	100.00
Wholesale and retail	11.95	66.84	12.09	4.36	1.51	0.88	0.58	0.28	0.26	0.23	1.02	100.00
Construction and building	2.67	57.32	26.43	7.80	2.21	0.86	0.89	0.36	0.12	0.16	1.19	100.00
Transport, storage, and communications	3.95	50.14	37.85	4.03	2.42	0.53	0.28	0.11	0.08	0.08	0.53	100.00
Finance and insurance services	1.93	45.58	26.90	9.44	3.86	1.93	1.62	1.12	0.61	0.71	6.29	100.00
Tourism	19.67	62.96	7.33	3.44	1.41	1.61	0.48	0.52	0.57	0.36	1.66	100.00
Other Services	23.71	60.37	8.14	3.14	1.26	0.69	0.44	0.38	0.34	0.31	1.22	100.00
Unclassified	9.03	70.82	14.53	2.47	1.05	0.59	0.25	0.27	0.12	0.17	0.70	100.00

Source: Social Security Corporation, computer section.

TABLE 5A.8
Frequency Distribution of Jordanian Workers Covered by Social Security According to Wage Group and Main Profession, Second Quarter 1987

Main Profession	Wage Groups (JD)											Total
	<50	50-	100-	150-	200-	250-	300-	350-	400-	450-	500+	
Professionals and technicians	905	10,987	6,656	2,012	940	523	452	350	221	194	360	23,600
Managers and administrative workers	14	109	150	170	178	174	124	132	86	98	385	1,620
Clerical staff	626	22,744	11,520	3,725	1,497	755	404	248	111	100	232	41,962
Salespersons	92	1,822	978	382	174	102	51	50	20	26	60	3,757
Workers in services	2,456	29,613	3,350	622	141	61	32	12	9	9	74	36,379
Workers in agriculture	194	12,042	825	188	30	19	2	7	1	2	24	13,334
Production and transport workers	7,785	58,495	27,073	8,437	2,663	908	364	192	88	54	237	106,296
Unclassified	1,659	14,122	7,312	4,135	2,977	1,639	849	588	416	407	1128	35,232
Total	13,731	149,934	57,864	19,671	8,600	4,181	2,278	1,579	952	890	2,500	262,180

Source: Social Security Corporation, computer section.

TABLE 5A.9

Frequency Distribution of Non-Jordanian Workers Covered by Social Security According to Wage Group and Main Profession, Second Quarter 1987

Main Profession	Wage Groups (JD)											Total
	<50	50-	100-	150-	200-	250-	300-	350-	400-	450-	500+	
Professionals and technicians	343	2,658	2,038	399	214	128	103	74	64	67	179	6,267
Managers and administrative workers	10	62	31	33	32	33	31	31	26	24	165	478
Clerical staff	317	3,355	1,230	450	225	111	91	54	24	20	93	5,970
Salespersons	70	640	163	63	21	21	8	9	10	9	11	1,025
Workers in services	7,147	18,705	968	207	84	49	20	19	26	16	78	27,319
Workers in agriculture	1,355	7,894	437	44	15	2	1	1	2	3	22	9,776
Production and transport workers	6,711	47,852	14,943	3,738	1,151	387	236	110	38	38	309	75,513
Unclassified	999	3,784	2,136	1,075	499	359	230	132	89	98	529	9,930
Total	16,952	84,950	21,946	6,009	2,241	1,090	720	430	279	275	1,386	136,278

Source: Social Security Corporation, computer section.

TABLE 5A.10
Frequency Distribution of Jordanian Workers Covered by Social Security According to Wage Group and Sex, Second Quarter 1987

Sex	Wage Groups (JD)											Total
---	<50	50-	100-	150-	200-	250-	300-	350-	400-	450-	500+	
Male	8,714	125,086	51,188	17,682	7,826	3,869	2,158	1,497	913	859	2,412	222,204
Female	4,912	24,178	6,564	1,948	756	305	116	80	38	31	86	39,014
Unclassified	105	670	112	41	18	7	4	2	1	0	2	962
Total	13,731	149,934	57,864	19,671	8,600	4,181	2,278	1,579	952	890	2,500	262,180

Source: Social Security Corporation, computer section.

TABLE 5A.11
Frequency Distribution of Non-Jordanian Workers Covered by Social Security According to Wage Group and Sex, Second Quarter 1987

| | Wage Groups (JD) | | | | | | | | | | | | |
Sex	<50	50-	100-	150-	200-	250-	300-	350-	400-	450-	500+	Total
Male	15,718	80,793	20,531	5,260	1,999	975	651	384	256	249	1,342	128,158
Female	1,053	3,685	1,321	716	231	110	67	44	22	26	39	7,314
Unclassified	181	472	94	33	11	5	2	2	1	0	5	806
Total	16,952	84,950	21,946	6,009	2,241	1,090	720	430	279	275	1,386	136,278

Source: Social Security Corporation, computer section.

TABLE 6A.1
Number of Wage Earners in Establishments with Five Employees or More by Sex and Economic Activity, 1980-1986

Sector	1980 M	1980 F	1981 M	1981 F	1982 M	1982 F	1983 M	1983 F	1984 M	1984 F	1985 M	1985 F	1986 M	1986 F
Mining and quarrying	5,827	35	2,091	41	6,363	62	6,626	60	6,628	75	6,083	94	6,484	96
Manufacturing	12,242	1,231	17,768	1,916	16,900	1,824	17,195	1,859	17,686	2,101	23,429	2,822	20,630	2,500
Electricity, gas, and water	1,963	38	2,427	58	3,704	96	3,571	121	3,968	121	4,284	148	4,371	172
Construction	2,848	81	2,775	76	2,756	72	2,999	82	5,422	157	5,534	186	3,745	176
Commerce	6,728	543	6,438	398	7,411	503	7,314	471	8,734	673	9,161	645	8,686	642
Transport and storage	2,092	162	6,109	838	6,707	971	7,012	965	7,368	983	9,390	1,028	8,657	969
Financial services	3,998	1,399	3,458	1,371	5,444	2,369	5,648	2,447	6,312	2,644	6,784	2,797	6,692	2,719
Comm. sevices and public administration	57,607	20,993	58,615	19,812	66,304	22,278	64,771	22,972	62,101	28,268	63,534	28,091	75,257	32,621
Total	93,305	24,482	99,681	24,510	115,319	28,175	115,136	28,977	118,216	35,022	128,199	35,811	134,524	39,895
Female percentage	20.8		19.7		19.6		20.1		22.8		21.8		22.9	

Source: Department of Statistics, Employment Survey (various issues).

TABLE 6A.2
Numbers of University Graduates Employed in Establishments with Five Employees or More by Economic Activity, 1980-1986

Sector	1980 M	1980 F	1981 M	1981 F	1982 M	1982 F	1983 M	1983 F	1984 M	1984 F	1985 M	1985 F	1986 M	1986 F
Mining and quarrying	258	4	90	3	344	14	351	13	370	21	412	23	467	22
Manufacturing	547	28	903	46	1,016	61	1,025	66	1,211	69	1,239	69	1,144	80
Electricity, gas, and water	78	3	189	2	351	9	375	17	430	18	491	28	506	36
Construction	312	7	306	5	343	16	339	17	619	33	578	34	569	35
Commerce	453	46	403	22	497	36	436	28	722	65	770	85	802	86
Transport and storage	129	16	527	148	658	193	650	207	701	210	779	234	780	249
Financial services	922	168	797	159	1,186	315	1255	335	1,448	387	1,544	406	1618	426
Comm. services and public administration	11,490	2,518	10,642	2,299	12,961	3,290	13,740	3,750	14,302	4,760	13,962	5,143	17,039	6,346
Total	14,191	2,790	13,857	2,684	17,356	3,934	18,171	4,433	19,803	5,563	19,775	6,022	22,925	7,280
Female percentage	16.4		16.2		18.5		19.6		21.9		23.3		24.1	

Source: Department of Statistics, *Employment Survey* (various issues).

TABLE 6A.3
Average Monthly Wage of all Employees by Major Activity, 1980-1986 (JD)

Sector	1980 M	1980 F	1981 M	1981 F	1982 M	1982 F	1983 M	1983 F	1984 M	1984 F	1985 M	1985 F	1986 M	1986 F
Mining and quarrying	135.0	111.0	149.8	105.3	179.8	141.5	203.9	149.3	222.3	182.6	205.6	146.6	213.1	160.9
Manufacturing	96.0	57.0	97.7	62.7	129.2	78.0	134.7	84.3	140.8	81.0	133.0	75.4	130.8	81.7
Electricity, gas, and water	99.0	74.0	112.7	82.4	104.2	85.2	141.5	117.5	132.9	120.3	151.4	120.2	156.2	128.8
Construction	137.0	121.0	135.5	126.3	164.8	198.3	158.8	194.7	176.8	176.7	171.0	175.0	198.9	175.0
Commerce	101.0	91.0	107.5	108.3	125.2	122.8	128.4	124.8	147.3	136.9	145.8	149.3	151.3	145.2
Transport and storage	114.0	125.0	149.2	163.8	140.8	97.7	168.4	165.6	171.0	249.9	170.6	173.5	169.1	140.9
Financial services	150.0	98.0	167.8	110.8	179.1	127.5	189.5	136.4	217.8	149.0	233.1	155.8	241.0	157.8
Comm. services and public administration	86.0	77.0	95.1	84.6	107	93.1	106.5	96.0	110.2	95.8	118.0	101.4	122.8	106.4

Source: Department of Statistics, *Employment Survey* (various issues).

TABLE 6A.4
Average Monthly Wage of Graduates by Major Activity, 1980-1986 (JD)

Sector	1980		1981		1982		1983		1984		1985		1986	
	M	F	M	F	M	F	M	F	M	F	M	F	M	F
Mining and quarrying	360.0	147.0	330.2	155.7	420.1	211.6	427.4	210.8	419.8	252.5	409.4	188.7	400.8	211.7
Manufacturing	258.0	147.0	250.9	154.8	326.9	204.3	340.0	267.7	360.7	219.4	375.4	234.7	358.8	244.2
Electricity, gas, and water	328.0	166.0	298.3	203.0	199.5	191.1	347.2	190.4	307.2	183.2	346.8	185.2	363.3	194.6
Construction	393.0	178.0	381.8	138.0	453.8	284.3	452.1	281.1	473.4	242.5	458.7	225.9	481.3	282.4
Commerce	218.0	122.0	244.6	165.1	274.5	170.1	286.0	168.6	321.2	219.6	331.8	220.0	331.7	239.5
Transport and storage	227.0	157.0	220.6	178.7	212.4	111.8	275.6	197.6	281.8	200.5	309.8	217.6	263.5	170.8
Financial Services	234.0	132.0	274.2	150.3	284.8	160.2	309.1	169.7	359.4	195.1	413.3	230.2	403.7	220.3
Comm. services and public administration	151.0	112.0	173.5	129.4	190.7	143.2	187.6	142.6	184.4	138.2	200.0	143.0	214.4	147.0

Source: Department of Statistics, *Employment Survey* (various issues).

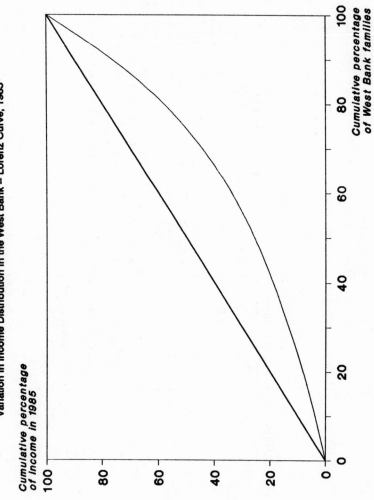

FIGURE 7A.1

Variation in Income Distribution in the West Bank – Lorenz Curve, 1985

Cumulative percentage
of Income in 1985

Cumulative percentage
of West Bank families

FIGURE 7A.2
Variation in Income Distribution in the Gaza Strip – Lorenz Curve, 1985

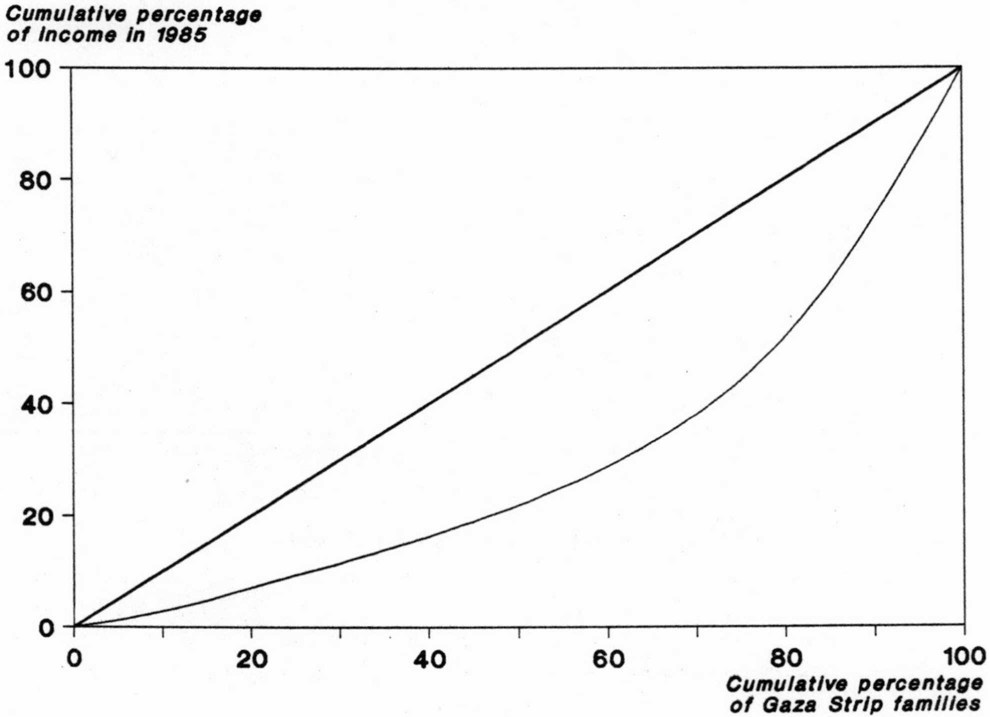

Cumulative percentage
of income in 1985
100
80
60
40
20
0
0
20
40
60
80
100
Cumulative percentage
of Gaza Strip families

TABLE 7.A1
Distribution of Families in West Bank and Gaza Strip According to Income and Residence, 1985

Family Level of Income (JD)	City		Village		Refugee Camp		Total	
	No.	%	No.	%	No.	%	No.	%
West Bank								
Top (more than 600)	17	85.00	2	10.00	1	5.00	20	2.73
Upper (401-600)	24	66.60	12	33.30	-	-	37	4.91
Middle (201-400)	92	57.80	54	33.90	13	8.10	159	21.72
Low (101-200)	80	40.20	97	48.70	22	11.00	199	27.20
Bottom (100 and less)	98	30.82	117	36.79	103	32.40	318	43.44

TABLE 7A.1 (continued)
Distribution of Families in West Bank and Gaza Strip According to Income and Residence, 1985

Family Level of Income (JD)	City		Village		Refugee Camp		Total	
	No.	%	No.	%	No.	%	No.	%
Gaza Strip								
Top (more than 600)	3	60.00	2	40.00	-	-	5	1.10
Upper (401-600)	9	56.20	3	18.70	4	25.00	16	3.53
Middle (201-400)	30	49.10	8	13.10	23	37.70	61	13.49
Low (101-200)	46	41.44	13	11.71	52	46.85	111	24.55
Bottom (100 and less)	134	51.74	29	11.20	96	31.10	259	57.30

TABLE 7A.1 (continued)
Distribution of Families in West Bank and Gaza Strip According to Income and Residence, 1985

Family Level of Income (JD)	City		Village		Refugee Camp		Total	
	No.	%	No.	%	No.	%	No.	%
West Bank and Gaza Strip								
Top (more than 600)	20	80.00	4	16.00	1	4.00	25	2.11
Upper (401-600)	33	63.40	15	28.80	4	8.60	52	4.39
Middle (201-400)	122	55.40	62	28.10	36	16.30	220	18.58
Low (101-200)	126	40.78	110	35.60	74	23.62	310	26.18
Bottom (100 and less)	232	40.30	146	25.30	199	34.30	577	48.73

Source: Abu Shokor, A.F.: "Social Structure and Pattern of Income Distribution in the West Bank and Gaza Strip," Nablus: An-Najah National University, January 1987, unpublished.

TABLE 7A.2
Income Distribution in the West Bank and Gaza Strip According to Employment Status of Head of Family, 1985

Employment Status	Bottom Income No.	Bottom Income %	Low Income No.	Low Income %	Middle Income No.	Middle Income %	Upper Income No.	Upper Income %	Top Income No.	Top Income %	Total No.	Total %
West Bank												
Self-Employed	85	29.10	75	25.68	89	30.47	30	10.27	13	4.45	292	40.10
Employed	190	53.22	104	29.13	55	15.40	4	1.12	4	1.12	357	49.03
Unemployed	40	50.62	20	25.31	14	17.72	2	2.53	3	3.79	79	10.85
Gaza Strip												
Self-Employed	92	45.32	59	29.06	36	17.73	11	5.41	5	3.46	203	45.21
Employed	137	66.18	44	21.25	23	11.11	3	1.44			27	46.10
Unemployed	28	71.79	7	17.94	2	5.12	2	5.12			39	8.68
West Bank and Gaza Strip												
Self-Employed	177	35.75	134	27.07	125	25.25	41	8.28	18	3.63	495	42.05
Employed	327	57.97	148	26.24	78	13.82	7	1.24	4	0.70	564	47.91
Unemployed	68	57.62	27	22.88	16	13.55	4	3.38	3	2.54	118	10.02

Source: Abu Shokor, A.F.: "Social Structure and Pattern of Income Distribution in the West Bank and Gaza Strip," Nablus: An-Najah National University, January 1987, unpublished.

TABLE 7A.3
Sources of Income for Different Income Groups in the West Bank and Gaza Strip, 1985

Source of Income	Bottom Income		Low Income		Middle Income		Upper Income		Top Income		Total	
	No.	%	No.	%	No.	%	No.	%	No.	%	No.	%
West Bank												
Agriculture	53	16.35	62	31.16	46	28.93	11	30.56	6	30.00	177	24.18
Industry	48	15.09	32	16.08	22	13.84	10	27.78	2	10.00	104	14.21
Construction	66	20.75	26	13.07	23	14.47	5	13.89	2	10.00	122	16.67
Trade	56	17.61	31	15.08	37	23.27	17	47.22	8	40.00	149	20.36
Transportation	19	5.97	16	0.04	13	8.18	1	2.78			49	6.69
Rents of houses or lands	40	12.50	39	19.60	38	23.90	7	19.44	7	35.00	131	17.90
Private and public services	55	17.29	67	33.67	51	32.08	10	28.78	5	25.00	188	25.68
Israeli labor-market	26	8.18	30	15.08	25	15.72			3	15.00	84	11.48
Transfers from abroad	14	4.40									14	1.91
Retirement	3	0.94	6	3.02	4	2.52					13	1.78
Social welfare	10	3.14									10	1.37
Zakah	14	4.40									14	1.91
National insurance	1	0.31	1	0.50							2	0.27
Old-age pensions	1	0.31			1	0.38					2	0.27

TABLE 7A.3 (continued)
Sources of Income for Different Income Groups in the West Bank and Gaza Strip, 1985

Source of Income	Bottom Income		Low Income		Middle Income		Upper Income		Top Income		Total	
	No.	%	No.	%	No.	%	No.	%	No.	%	No.	%
Gaza Strip												
Agriculture	30	11.58	14	12.61	8	13.11	3	18.75	3	60.00	58	12.83
Industry	52	20.08	33	29.73	13	21.31	4	25.00			102	22.57
Construction	61	23.55	25	22.02	6	9.84	1	6.25			93	20.58
Trade	44	16.99	25	22.02	20	32.79	6	37.50	2	40.00	97	21.46
Transportation	11	4.25	13	11.71	8	13.11	1	6.25			33	7.30
Rents of houses or lands	25	9.65	17	15.32	10	16.39	5	31.25	2	40.00	59	5.53
Private and public services	38	14.67	19	17.12	24	39.34	3	18.75	1	20.00	85	18.81
Israeli labor-market	5	1.93	13	11.71	13	21.31	1	6.25			32	7.08
Transfers from abroad	17	6.56	6	5.41	4	6.06	2	12.50			29	6.41
Retirement	2	0.77	1	0.90	1	1.64	1	6.25			5	1.11
Social welfare	3	1.16									3	0.66
Zakah	2	0.77									2	0.44
National insurance												
Old-age pensions												

TABLE 7A.3 (continued)
Sources of Income for Different Income Groups in the West Bank and Gaza Strip, 1985

Source of Income	Bottom Income		Low Income		Middle Income		Upper Income		Top Income		Total	
	No.	%	No.	%	No.	%	No.	%	No.	%	No.	%
West Bank and Gaza Strip												
Agriculture	82	14.21	76	24.52	45	24.55	14	26.92	9	32.00	235	19.85
Industry	100	17.33	65	20.97	35	15.91	14	26.92	2	8.00	206	17.40
Construction	127	22.01	51	16.45	69	13.18	6	11.54	2	8.00	215	18.16
Trade	100	17.33	56	18.06	57	25.91	23	44.23	10	40.00	246	20.78
Transportation	30	5.20	29	9.36	21	9.45	2	3.85			82	6.93
Rents of houses or lands	65	11.27	56	18.06	48	21.82	12	23.08	9	36.00	190	16.05
Private and public services	94	16.12	86	27.74	75	34.09	13	25	6	24.00	273	23.06
Israeli labor-market	31	5.37	43	13.87	38	17.27	1	1.92	3	12.00	116	9.80
Transfers from abroad	31	5.37	6	1.94	4	1.82	2	3.85			47	3.97
Retirement	5	0.87	1	0.32	5	2.27	1	1.92			18	1.52
Social welfare	13	2.25									13	1.10
Zakah	16	2.77									16	1.35
National insurance	1	0.17	1	0.32							2	0.17
Old-age pensions	1	0.17			1	0.45					2	0.17

Source: Abu Shokor, A.F.: "Social Structure and Pattern of Income Distribution in the West Bank and Gaza Strip,"Nablus: An-Najah National University, January 1987, unpublished.

TABLE 7A.4
Distribution of Family Income in the West Bank and Gaza Strip by Economic Activity, 1985

Economic Activity	Bottom Income		Low Income		Middle Income		Upper Income		Top Income		Total	
	No.	%	No.	%	No.	%	No.	%	No.	%	No.	%
West Bank												
Unemployed	42	13.21	20	10.05	13	8.18	1	2.77	3	15.00	79	10.80
Agriculture	30	9.43	18	9.05	15	9.43	2	5.56	1	5.00	66	9.02
Industry	46	14.47	26	13.07	13	8.18	6	16.67	2	10.00	93	12.72
Construction	57	17.92	18	9.05	18	11.32	3	8.33	1	5.00	97	13.26
Public service	46	14.46	44	22.11	33	20.75	6	16.67	2	10.00	131	17.92
Transportation	12	3.77	11	5.53	8	5.05	1	2.77			32	4.37
Private service	32	11.33	34	17.09	28	17.61	1	2.77	3	15.00	102	13.85
Trade	49	15.41	27	13.57	31	19.49	16	44.44	8	40.00	131	17.92

TABLE 7A.4 (continued)
Distribution of Family Income in the West Bank and Gaza Strip by Economic Activity, 1985

Economic Activity	Bottom Income		Low Income		Middle Income		Upper Income		Top Income		Total	
	No.	%	No.	%	No.	%	No.	%	No.	%	No.	%
Gaza Strip												
Unemployed	29	11.20	7	3.31	2	3.28	2	12.50			40	8.87
Agriculture	21	8.11	5	4.51	3	4.92	1	6.25	2	40.00	32	7.01
Industry	50	19.31	26	23.42	9	14.75	2	12.50			87	19.29
Construction	55	21.24	18	16.22	3	4.92					76	16.85
Public service	29	11.20	12	10.81	16	26.23	3	18.75			60	13.30
Transportation	10	3.86	7	6.31	3	4.92					20	4.43
Private service	26	10.04	14	12.61	9	14.75	2	12.25	2	40.00	53	11.75
Trade	39	15.06	21	18.92	16	26.23	6	37.50	1	20.00	83	10.40

TABLE 7A.4 (continued)
Distribution of Family Income in the West Bank and Gaza Strip by Economic Activity, 1985

Economic Activity	Bottom Income		Low Income		Middle Income		Upper Income		Top Income		Total	
	No.	%	No.	%	No.	%	No.	%	No.	%	No.	%
West Bank and Gaza Strip												
Unemployed	71	12.30	27	8.71	15	6.82	3	5.77	3	12.00	119	10.08
Agriculture	51	8.84	23	7.42	18	8.18	3	5.77	3	12.00	98	8.29
Industry	97	16.64	52	16.77	22	10.00	8	15.39	2	8.00	180	15.23
Construction	112	19.41	36	11.61	21	9.55	3	5.77	1	4.00	123	14.64
Public service	75	13.00	56	18.07	49	22.27	9	17.31	2	8.00	191	16.16
Transportation	22	3.81	18	5.81	11	5.00	1	1.92			52	4.40
Private service	62	10.75	48	15.48	27	16.82	3	5.77	5	20.00	155	13.11
Trade	88	15.25	48	15.48	47	21.36	22	42.31	9	36.00	214	18.10

Source: Abu Shokor, A.F.: "Social Structure and Pattern of Income Distribution in the West Bank and Gaza Strip,"Nablus: An-Najah National University, January 1987, unpublished.

TABLE 9A.1
Social Security Scheme

Circumstance	Coverage	Source of Funds	Qualifying Conditions
Old age, invalidity, death [a]	Employees older than 16, including those in private establishments with 5 or more workers; government and employees of universities and municipalities not covered by government pensions. Exclusions: Agricultural employees, seamen, fishermen, domestic servants, the self-employed, family labor, and some foreign employees.	Insured person: 5% of wage. Employer: 8% of payroll. Government: any deficit. (Insured worker can contribute additional amounts to receive credit for previous periods, periods of employment not covered).	Old-age pension: age 60 (men), 55 (women), and 120 months coverage (of which 36 months continuous within last 5 years) or 15 years intermittent coverage. Invalidity pension: total incapacity for work and 12 months continuous coverage or 24 months intermittent coverage. Survivor pension: deceased had 12 months of continuous coverage or 24 months intermittent coverage.
Work injury [a]	Employees older than 16, including those in private establishments with 5 or more workers; government and public sector employees; and employees of universities and municipalities not covered by government pensions. Exclusions: Agricultural employees, seamen, fishermen, domestic servants, the self-employed, family labor, and some foreign employees.	Insured person: zero %. Employer: 2% of payroll (may be reduced to 1% if employer assumes full cost of medical treatment and disbursement of daily allowances for temporary disability). Government: zero %.	Work injury benefits: no minimum qualifying period.

a First and current law, 1978; social insurance system.
b Except permanent disability.

TABLE 9A.1 (continued)

Circumstance	Cash Benefits for Insured Worker [b]	Permanent Disability/ Medical Benefits for Insured Worker	Survivor Benefits/ Medical Benefits for Dependents
Old age, invalidity, death	Old age pension: 2% of average monthly wages in last 2 years multiplied by number of years of contribution. Maximum: 75% of average monthly wage. Pension increased by 10% for 1st dependent and 5% each for 2nd and 3rd. Reduced pensions available at age 46 (15 years coverage) and for those not covered or who have left the country. Lump-sum equal to 15% of average wages last 2 years for each year of contribution if ineligible for pension.	Invalidity pension: 50% of average monthly wage in last year of contribution times degree of disability. Constant-attendance allowance: pension increased by 25%.	Survivor pension: 50% of last year's earnings if eligible for pension at death. If pensioner at death, full pension is paid to widow, children (under 18, 26 if student, no age limit if invalid), unmarried daughters, or dependent parents, brothers, and sisters. Pension reduced in direct proportion to survivor's income. Widow's, daughter's, or sister's pension right forfeited upon marriage.
Work injury	Temporary disability benefit (industrial accident): 75% of daily wage (65% if receiving treatment in specified medical institutions) for duration of disability until permanent disability is proved or upon death.	Permanent disability pension (industrial accident): 75% of covered monthly wage. Constant-attendance allowance: pension increased by 25%. Partial disability: if 30% or more disability, percentage of full disability pension according to degree of disability. If less than 30%, same but paid as lump-sum equal to 36 months pension. Medical benefits (work injury): medical treatment, medicines, hospitalization, and transportation.	Survivor pension (industrial accident): 60% of covered monthly wage, paid to widow, dependent widower, orphans younger than 16, and other qualified dependents.

TABLE 10A.1
Health Care Expenditures by Sources (million JD)

Year	MOH	Insurance Fees	JUH	RMS	Private Sector	UNRWA	Total	GNP in Current Market Prices	Per Capita Health Care Expenditure (JD)	Ratio of Health Care Expenditure to GNP (%)
1978	9.943	0.344[a]	2.305	6.500	15.32[b]	0.74[c]	35.152	781.00	17.080	4.50
1979	13.234	0.871	4.027	6.750	18.47[a]	0.81	44.797	921.30	21.000	4.86
1980	14.062	1.000[a]	4.5[b]	9.700	20.20	0.96	50.422	1190.10	22.730	4.20
1981	14.666	1.187	4.950	10.900	26.10	0.89	58.693	1482.70	25.440	3.96
1982	20.000	1.410	4.858	12.400	28.60	0.96	68.228	1673.40	28.440	4.08
1983	20.290	1.560	5.131	14.000	31.00	1.07	73.051	1770.30	29.280	4.13
1984	20.296	1.760	7.442	15.800	34.00	1.18	80.478	1853.60	31.010	4.34
1985	27.200	2.070	8.761	17.806	37.00	1.30	94.131	1881.8[d]	34.950	5.09
1986	31.330	2.440	10.296	19.150	40.49	1.30	105.000	1919.4[d]	37.550	5.49

a These figures consist of hospital and health centers insurance fees, while premiums are included in the ministry's budget.
b Estimated point.
c Estimated by the author.
d Preliminary.

Sources: Department of Planning, Ministry of Health, *Statistical Annual Reports, 1977-1986* (Amman, n.d.); Central Bank of Jordan, *Monthly Statistical Bulletin* 24 (April 1988), p. 70.

Appendix B

Jordan's Economy: Some Basic Facts

Matthes Buhbe

1. Background

The modern history of Jordan is linked to the decline of Ottoman rule over the Arab East. The Arab Revolt, which began in 1916 under the leadership of the Hashemite Sherif Hussein of Mecca, was one of the catalysts for the breakup of the Ottoman Empire, the last multinational Muslim domain in the history of Islam. In the aftermath of World War I, Abdallah, son of Sherif Hussein, founded the Emirate of Transjordan. It was transformed into the Hashemite Kingdom of Jordan after World War II.

Today, the country's northern, eastern, and southern borders are with Syria, Iraq, and Saudi Arabia, respectively. The River Jordan and the Wadi Araba rift form the western border since the kingdom's decision on July 31, 1988, to disengage from the Israeli-occupied parts of Palestine.

Geopolitical facts influenced Jordan's economic development. In the assessment of the kingdom's crown prince, "The impact of geography on the political economy of the region is especially apparent in the area that comprises modern Jordan, lying as it does between the fertile crescent and the arid desert, where the age-old struggle between the desert and the sown continues to the present day" (Bin Talal, 1984, p.73). He continued: "Historically, Jordan attained most of its importance because it was part of a wider area; it was the hinge, so to speak, that linked the sharply contrasted zones that lay to north and south, east and west. The political developments that began with the advent of the twentieth century once again placed Jordan at the center of events, and brought into high relief its potential role as a middle ground, in more senses than one, in the Arab East" (Bin Talal, 1984, p.75).

The political economy of Jordan is also influenced by ancient and new dimensions in availability of resources. Water resources and rain-fed areas west of the desert support agriculture and population increase, but these are limited, as are other natural resources. Although the exploitation of Jordan's water, mineral, and trade resources in the modern era can be found in ancient times, the modern demographic dimension cannot. Within the context both of the Arab-Israeli conflict and the oil boom in neighboring countries, Jordan has had to cope with extreme dynamics in population change. According to the crown prince, the population of both the East and West Bank of the Jordan River "stood at less than one million people on the eve of the first Arab-Israeli war in 1946. This settled population was augmented by 42 per cent during 1948" through the inflow of Palestinian refugees to both Banks (Bin Talal, 1984, p.91). The 1961 census enumer-

TABLE B.1
Indicators of Jordan's Economic Development, 1952-1988

Indicators	Annual Averages					
	1952-66	1967-72	1973-80	1981-85	1987	1988
Real growth rates (%)						
GDP at market prices	6.9	4.6	10.9	4.2	3.0	-5.3
Per capita income (GNP)	4.4	-	7.5	0.4	-6.3	-9.9
GDP ratios (%)						
Domestic demand [a]	126.2	135.7	155.4	175.4	129.7	129.4
Commodity exports	17.5 [b]	12.8	11.5	14.6	14.8	19.1
Commodity imports	42.1 [b]	49.6	83.3	68.0	54.3	60.1
Public expenditure	30.7	54.6	61.3	51.2	57.3	61.4
Currency value						
Cost of living [c]	-	29.8	76.9	100.0	100.3	117.6
U.S.-$/J.D. [d]	-	2.8	3.2	2.5	2.9	2.1
Domestic labor force						
Participation rate [e]	24.0	-	22.0	20.2	19.2	19.1

[a] Consumption and gross investment, private and public.
[b] Including services.
[c] Index for 1985=100. End of period values. Index March 1989=125.8.
[d] Exchange rates at the end of period; March 1989: 1.85 U.S.-$/J.D.
[e] Economically active Jordanians in % of Jordanian population.

Sources: Central Bank of Jordan, *Yearly Statistical Series, 1964-1983* (Amman, 1984); Central Bank of Jordan, *Monthly Statistical Bulletin* 25 (2) (Amman, February 1989); Department of Statistics, Statistical Yearbook, 1987 (Amman, n.d.); Ministry of Planning, *Five Year Plan 1986-1990* (Amman, 1986).

ated 0.8 million inhabitants in the West Bank and 0.9 million in the East Bank. The 1967 occupation of the West Bank by Israel resulted in relative stagnation in the size of the West Bank population, while at the same time the East Bank population more than tripled. In 1987, the estimated population of the East Bank stood at 2.9 million (Department of Statistics, Statistical Yearbook, 1987, p.13).

The high standard of education and professional skills of the Palestinian-Jordanian population proved an essential economic asset to Jordan from the beginning of the oil boom in neighboring Arab countries. Demand-pull factors for skilled labor resulted in emigration from both banks in huge numbers. "Our investment in education, manpower development and social services since 1948 has done more than help to alleviate the consequences of the major human tragedy that afflicted the Arabs of Palestine; but the economic growth of the area as a whole has benefited by providing the skilled manpower resources badly needed by oil countries, where about 400,000 Jordanian nationals are employed today" (Bin Talal, 1984, p.92). Although remittances from this labor force "have helped towards meeting our chronic foreign trade deficit, the costs to the country have been substantial in terms of the drain on the best of our skilled manpower resources" (Bin Talal, 1984, p.92).

The impact of demographic factors on Jordan's political economy cannot be overestimated. From 1980 to 1986, the annual rate of population growth was estimated at 3.7% (World Bank, 1988, p. 275). If this growth were to be sustained, Jordan's number of inhabitants would double every twenty years. Another implication is the high dependency ratio per economically active Jordanian. A low female participation rate in the labor force and an age structure in which half the population is younger than fifteen years have resulted in a ratio of about five dependents per income earner. Currently, the average family size is approximately seven persons (6.7 according to Chapter 2 or 7.2 according to Chapter 8).

2. Economic Structure and Growth

Some key factors in Jordan's political economy are an orientation toward transport, trade, and services; a limited endowment of natural resources (mainly phosphate, potash, and limestone); a narrow agricultural base (only 5% of the land is arable); and a remarkable demography with a high influx of refugees, high labor immigration, even higher labor emigration, and a high rate of population increase.

Before discussing structural characteristics, let me introduce some major economic indicators. Most prominent are annual rates of real growth of gross domestic product (GDP) and per capita income. On average, Jordan has witnessed tremendous economic growth, as shown in the first two rows of Table B.1. This growth path slowed in the aftermath of the 1967 war with Israel and in recent years after the end of the oil boom in neighboring Arab countries. The recession in the 1980s led to zero growth, and even to a decline, in per capita income (measured in terms of gross national product [GNP]).

Such dynamic domestic economic expansion involves external factors as well as a sound internal development strategy. Two external factors are the remittances of Jordanians working abroad and the financial assistance of Arab and other non-Jordanian donors. In Jordan, public expenditure amounts to more than 50% of GDP (row 6 in Table B.1), and a substantial share is financed from abroad. In some years, grants and development loans amounted to one-half of government revenue. These funds were used mainly for development projects. On average, one-third of the government's budget is spent on capital formation--to a large extent, investment in economic and social development. Two-thirds of the budget are consumption expenditure. These government activities form part of Jordan's total consumption and gross investment (row 3 in Table B.1). They clearly add up to much more than 100% of GDP. This is made possible by a considerable external deficit in the trade of goods and services. Commodity imports alone frequently rose above 60% of GDP (row 5 in Table B.1). Imports of goods and services exceeded GDP in several years (for example, from 1979 to 1984). At the same time total exports barely reached one-half of the size of the imports. Domestic commodity exports never reached one-third of commodity imports (rows 4 and 5 in Table B.1). The trade gap was financed to a large extent by remittances. In 1984, reported remittances of Jordanians working abroad reached a record ratio of 36.1% of GDP at factor cost.

Clearly, rising public expenditure and rising remittances were important demand-pull factors vitalizing Jordan's domestic economy. Nevertheless, many of the demanded goods and services were not available at home and required increasing imports. Imports can be used for consumption or for investment in the domestic capital stock. Until 1985, the composition of commodity imports showed a relative decline in consumer goods in favor of capital goods and raw materials. Continuation of such a trend would be desirable, since it would indicate a tendency toward investment instead of consumption of foreign products. The present recessionary climate does not allow high expansion of production capacity, which thus decreases the demand for imported capital goods. Nevertheless, imports for investements purposes have to increase again. Jordan needs to build up and enlarge domestic production in order to support the current standard of living for its growing population.

In this respect, Jordan has passed through various stages in development and development planning (see Chapter 1). It is sufficient to comment here on the domestic structure of economic activities between 1975 and 1987 (Table B.2).

The services sector accounted for the larger part of GDP. It was also the major employer. In 1986, the government's share in the employment of Jordanian nationals domestically was 47% (Smadi, 1987, p. 24). Private services accounted for another 23%. Only 30% were employed in the commodity-producing sectors (Smadi, 1987, p. 24).

By and large, Table B.2 indicates a stable production structure. There were no significant shifts from services to commodity production or any dramatic changes in commodity production itself. In 1983, by the end of the boom period, manufacturing and construction had expanded their share. Since then, however, their share has shrunk again to the preboom levels of 1975.

It is interesting to note that a structural change would have taken place had the sectoral price levels been invariant to each other. In constant 1975 prices (using the GNP deflator developed by the Central Bank of Jordan), the relative importance of mining and quarrying would have more than doubled in the period 1975-1987, and agriculture would also have risen significantly in importance. The shares of manufacturing and construction would have remained almost constant, leading to an increase in the GDP share of the commodity-producing sectors from 34.4% in 1975 to 45.5% in 1987. Relative prices developed in disfavor of commodity production, particularly mining and agriculture. Pressure from world markets in raw materials and food are believed to have created this inflation differential. Accordingly, international competition was less challenging for Jordan's manufacturing and construction industries. Least pressure was felt in the

TABLE B.2
Relative Importance of Economic Sectors in Jordan, 1975-1987[a]

Sectors	1975	1979	1983	1987
All services	65.6	63.3	61.3	63.7
All commodities	34.4	36.7	38.7	36.3
Agriculture	8.6	6.5	8.9	8.8
Mining and quarrying	5.4	4.1	3.1	4.5
Manufacturing	13.1	14.1	14.2	12.9
Electricity and water	1.0	1.5	2.3	3.1
Construction	6.3	10.5	10.2	7.0

[a] Economic activites as a percentage of GDP at factor cost in current prices.

Source: Buhbe, M., and Zreigat, S. (eds.): The Industrialization of Jordan (Amman: Royal Scientific Society, 1989).

services sector (Buhbe and Zreigat, 1989, p. 144).

3. Recent Developments

In the early 1980s, per capita income reached a record high. It climbed significantly above the U.S.-$ 2,000 mark and placed Jordan within the upper middle income category (World Bank classification). But an unfavorable combination of external and internal economic developments brought about a fall in per capita income. By 1987, it was less than $ 1,800, and 1988 was expected to show a considerably lower figure.

Recession spilled over from the neighboring Arab countries. Wage cuts and dismissals of Jordanians working abroad reflected negatively on remittances and added to unemployment in Jordan. More than that, Arab financial assistance to Jordan's government budget dwindled. In turn, Jordan borrowed foreign currency in rising amounts to sustain the level of public expenditure and commodity imports. Consequently, the dinar came

TABLE B.3
Relative Importance of Expenditure, 1983, 1985, and 1987[a]

	1983	1985	1987
Government consumption [b]	24.48	25.23	27.27
Private consumption	94.76	87.28	76.01
Changes in stocks	0.51	1.05	-
Private gross investment	20.66	15.07	6.48
Government gross investment [c]	14.68	14.39	19.97
Exports	44.79	48.45	44.69
Total expenditure	199.99	191.48	174.41
Imports	99.88	91.48	74.41
Gross domestic expenditure	100.00	100.00	100.00
Net factor income from abroad [d]	24.43	17.18	10.77
Gross national expenditure	124.43	117.18	110.77

[a] Expenditure on goods and services as a percentage of GDP at market price.
[b] "Recurrent expenditure" minus "repayment of loans for consumption purposes (internal and external, principal and interest)" minus "expenditure on durable consumer goods."
[c] "Capital expenditure" net of an estimated amount of repayments for development loans.
[d] Dominant items: "remittances from Jordanians working abroad" minus "remittances of guest workers in Jordan to their home countries."

Source: Central Bank of Jordan, *Annual Report, 1987* (Amman, 1988), pp. 4, 89.

under high devaluation pressure.

Throughout the past, import demand was supported by a strong and even overvalued Jordanian dinar, which was pegged to a basket of Western currencies (special drawing rights). The country's infant industries thus needed strong protection, and customs duties were the most important single source of domestic government revenue. At the same time, domestic exports were confronted by stiff international price competition.

The recessionary climate helped decrease Jordan's trade deficit. The relative importance of imports went down, as shown in Table B.3. Nevertheless, a sharp decrease in private expenditure contrasted with a considerable rise in public expenditure (Tables B.1 and B.3). In 1987, the public sector was the only major investor, and public expenditure was financed by a budget deficit as high as 18.4% of GDP or 16.6% of GNP (see Central Bank of Jordan, 1988, p. 37). The estimated deficit ratios regarding the 1988 budget were 18.7% and 17.0%, respectively. Therefore, despite decreasing imports, Jordan was forced to increase its external borrowing of funds.

The fundamentals of the Jordanian political economy did not seem fit for a Keynesian strategy of deficit spending. In October 1988, the country faced a severe shortage of foreign currency. This financial crisis forced a set of austerity measures on the economy, including import bans, devaluation of the dinar, and a rise in several administered prices. Government wages and salaries were frozen, and a further loss in real income per capita was inevitable.

4. Prospects

At the time of this writing, the country has not yet overcome its financial crisis. But the devaluation process had already lost momentum. This was partly due to previous price stability in Jordan. From 1985 to 1987, the cost of living index did not change. In 1988 and thereafter, only imported inflation as a direct result of devaluation was expected to take place. The rise in general price level thus is expected to be below the fall of the dinar against the dollar; this will eventually stop the devaluation-inflation process. If the dinar loses about 50% of its previous level against the dollar, a sufficent resistance against further devaluation is very likely. The present exchange rate is close to that level. The rise in general price levels has been below imported inflation and cuts in planned public expenditure (in real terms) for 1989 and 1990 are substantial. Imports are down and exports are up due to the increased price competitiveness of domestic industries and services. All this contributes to a new foreign currency market equilibrium. Of course, the recent sharp increase in external public debt contributed considerably to Jordan's financial crisis. A significant and sustained drop in net borrowing is, therefore, required to help reach equilibrium.

What remains to be solved is the dual problem of domestic recession and rising unemployment. Despite the availability of cheaper labor, the business climate is still down. Jordan has to rebuild its economic strength through a sharp and sustainable increase in gross investment. The decrease in labor costs is an important incentive for private investors. Nevertheless, there are other important economic and sociopolitical criteria. Public capital expenditure has to be kept at low levels in order not to repeat the trap of deficit spending of recent years. Private savings from inside Jordan and from abroad have to be channeled into new domestic activities. Instead of absorption through privatization of already established public enterprises, private funds have to be attracted by a competitive private sector under stable laws and cooperative capital-labor relations. Thus, private investment has to take the lead. Economic policy decisions can create appropriate incentives. There are many promising fields, and not all of them need capital-intensive production processes. By utilizing its well-educated work force, Jordan can extend production to regional needs, particularly those of the member states of the newly formed Arab Cooperation Council (Egypt, Iraq, Jordan, North Yemen) and of the Gulf Cooperation Council (Arabian peninsula). The devaluation of the dinar has already increased the competitiveness of Jordanian products and services. Jordan may become a science and technology center for the Arab East. Modern services, including maintenance and engineering consultancy to capital-intensive production lines abroad, are a promising field.

To sum up, the second half of the 1980s should not be allowed completely to overshadow the kingdom's remarkable success in earlier phases of economic development. Mistakes and failures are an inevitable by-product of dynamic growth and structural change. Lessons will be drawn, and in a few years Jordan may again be in the middle of a success story.

Bibliography

Bin Talal, Hassan: *Search for Peace*. London: Macmillan, 1984.
Buhbe, M., and Zreigat, S. (eds.): *The Industrialization of Jordan--Achievements and Obstacles*. Amman: Royal Scientific Society, 1989.
Central Bank of Jordan: *Yearly Statistical Series, 1964-1983*. Amman, 1984.
_____: *Annual Report, 1987*. Amman, 1988.
_____: *Monthly Statistical Bulletin 25* (2) (February 1989)..
Department of Statistics: *Statistical Yearbook, 1987*. Amman, n.d.
Ministry of Planning: *Five Year Plan for Economic and Social Development, 1986-*

1990. Amman, 1986.

Smadi, Mohammad et al.: *The Unemployment Problem in Jordan--Characteristics and Prospects.* Amman: Royal Scientific Society, November 1987.

World Bank: *World Development Report, 1988.* New York: Oxford University Press, 1988.

Bibliography

Abu Jaber, Kamel (ed.): *Major Issues in Jordanian Development*. Amman: Queen Alia Social Welfare Fund, 1983.

Abu Jaber, Kamel, Gharaibeh, Fawzi, and Hill, Allen: *The Badia of Jordan*. Amman: University of Jordan Press, 1987.

Abu Sheikha, A.: "Income Distribution and Poverty in Jordan." In Abu Jaber, Kamel (ed.): *Major Issues in Jordanian Development*. Amman: Queen Alia Social Welfare Fund, 1983.

Abu Shokor, A.F.: "Social Structure and Pattern of Income Distribution in the West Bank and Gaza Strip." Nablus: An-Najah National University, January 1987, unpublished.

_____: "Labor Market in the West Bank and Gaza Strip." Nablus: An-Najah National University, February 1987, unpublished.

_____: *Social and Economic Conditions of the Workers of the West Bank and Gaza Strip in Israel*. Nablus: An-Najah National University, April 1987.

Adelman, I., and Morris, C.T.: *Economic Growth and Social Equity in Developing Countries*. Stanford, Calif.: Stanford University Press, 1973.

Adelman, I., and Robinson, S.: *Income Distribution Policy in Developing Countries: A Case Study of Korea*. Oxford: Oxford University Press, 1978.

Ahluwalia, M.S.: "Income Distribution and Development: Some Stylized Facts." *American Economic Review* 66 (2) (1976), pp. 128-135.

Anand, S.: *Inequality and Poverty in Malaysia: Measurement and Decomposition*. New York: Oxford University Press, 1983.

Assaf, G.: *The Size Distribution of Income in Jordan 1973*. Amman: Royal Scientific Society, June 1979 (draft).

Atkinson, A.B.: "On Measurement of Inequality." *Journal of Economic Theory* 28 (3) (1970).

_____: *The Economics of Inequality*. Oxford: Clarendon Press, 1975.

Bin Talal, Hassan: *Search for Peace*. London: Macmillan, 1984.

Benvenisti, Meron: *Demographic, Economic, Legal, Social, and Political Developments in the West Bank: 1986 Report*. Boulder, Colo.: Westview Press, 1986.

Ben-Yosef, T.: " Analysis of Earnings Differentials Between Men and Women in Israel." Paper no. 7610. Jerusalem: Falle Institute, 1971.

Bohnet, Michael, and Betz, Rupert:: *Einkommensverteilung in Entwicklungslaendern*. Munich, 1976.

Buhbe, Matthes, and Zreigat, Sami (eds.): *Industrialization of Jordan—Achievements and Obstacles*. Amman: Royal Scientific Society, 1989.

Central Bank of Jordan: *Monthly Statistical Bulletin*. Amman: various issues.

_____: *Yearly Statistical Series, 1964-1983*. Amman: Central Bank of Jordan, 1984.

_____: *Annual Report, 1987*. Amman: Central Bank of Jordan, 1988.

_____: *Twenty Fifth Annual Report, 1988*. Amman: Central Bank of Jordan, 1989.

Central Bureau of Statistics: *Statistical Abstract of Israel, 1978*. Jerusalem: Central Bureau of Statistics, 1978.

_____: *Statistical Abstract of Israel, 1983*. Jerusalem: Central Bureau of Statistics, 1983.

Chenery, H.B.: "The Structural Approach to Development   Policy." *American Economic Review* 65 (1975), pp. 310-316.

Chiplin, B., and Sloane, P.J.: "Male/Female Earnings Differences: A Further Analysis." *British Journal of Industrial Relations* (1976).

Cowell, A.F.: *Measuring Inequality*. Oxford: Oxford University Press, 1977.

Dajani, J.S.: "Poverty and Income Distribution in Jordan." *Banks of Jordan Magazine* 1 (1982).

Dasgupta, P., Sen, A.K., and Starrett, D.: "Notes on the Measurement of Inequality." *Journal of Economic Theory* 31 (2) (1973).

Department of Statistics: *National Accounts in Jordan 1959-1963, 1967-1977, 1978-1982, 1981-1986*. Amman, several years.

_____: *Family Expenditure Survey, 1980*. Amman, n.d.

_____: *Manpower Survey, 1982-1983*. 2 Vols. Amman, n.d.

_____: *Employment Survey, 1986*. Amman, n.d.

_____: *Household Expenditure and Income Survey 1986-1987*. Amman, n.d.

_____: *Price Section 1987*. Amman, n.d.

_____: *Statistical Yearbook 1987*. Amman, n.d.

_____: *Family Expenditure Survey, 1986*. Amman, unpublished 1988 draft).

Dixon, John (ed.): *Social Welfare in the Middle East*. London: Croom Helm, 1987.

Donald, S. et al: *Statistics: A Fresh Approach*. New York: McGraw-Hill, 1980.

Eastaugh, Steven R.: *Medical Economics and Health Finance*. Boston: Auburn House, 1981.

Enke, S.: "Population and Development: A General Model." *Quarterly Journal of Economics* (1963), pp. 331-349.

_____: "The Economic Consequences of Rapid Population Growth." *Economic Journal* 81 (1971), pp. 800-811.

Fanny, Ginor: *Socio-Economic Disparities in Israel*. Tel Aviv: University Publishing Projects, 1979.

Feldstein, J.P.: *Health Care Economics*. New York: Wiley, 1983.

Fellner, W., and Haley, B.F.: *Reading in the Theory of Income Distribution*. London: Allen and Uwin, 1961.

Fields, G.S.: *Poverty, Inequality and Development*. New   York: Cambridge University Press, 1980.

Findlay, Allen, and Samha, Musa: "Return Migration and Urban Change--A Jordanian Case Study." In King, Russel (eds.): *Return Migration and Regional Economic Problems*. London: Croom Helm, 1986.

Fletcher, M.E.: *Economics and Social Problems*. Boston: Houghton Mifflin, 1979.

Foster, J.E.: "On Economic Poverty: A Survey of Aggregate Measures."*Advances in Econometrics* 3 (1984), pp. 215-251.

_____: "Inequality Measurements." In Young,   Peyton (ed.): *Fair Allocations*,

American Mathematical Society Proceedings of Symposia in Applied Mathematics 33 (1985).

Foxley, A.: Income Distribution in Latin America. London, 1976.

Glewwe, P.: "The Distribution of Income in Sri Lanka in 1969-1970 and 1980-1981: A Decomposition Analysis." *Journal of Development Economics* 28 (1987).

Gregory, P., Compell, J., and Cheny, B.: " A Cost Inclusive Simultaneous Equation Model of Birth Rates." *Econometrica* 40 (2) (1972), pp. 188-201.

Gubser, P.: "New Institutions and Processes in a Traditional Setting: Examples from Al-Karak, Jordan." In Cantori, L.J., and Harik, I. (eds.): *Local Politics and Development in the Middle East.* Boulder, Colo.: Westview Press, 1984.

Haas, M.: *Husseins Koenigreich, Jordaniens Stellung im Nahen Osten.* Munich: Tuduv-Verlag, 1975.

Hagenaars, A.J.M.: *The Perception of Poverty.* New York: Oxford University Press, 1986.

Hirschmann, A.O.: *The Strategy of Economic Development.* New Haven, Conn.: Yale University Press, 1958.

Hubbard, R.G., and Judd, K.L.: "Social Security and Individual Welfare." *American Economic Review* 77 (1987).

International Social Security Association: *The Planning of Social Security.* Geneva: ISSA, 1971.

_____: *The Current Issues in Social Security Planning: Consepts and Techniques.* Geneva: ISSA, 1973.

_____: *Methods of Evaluating the Effectiveness of Social Security Programmes.* Geneva: ISSA, 1976.

_____: *International Conference of Social Security Actuaries and Statisticians.* Mexico: ISSA, 1979.

Jordan Development Board: *Seven Year Program for Economic Development, 1964-1970.* Amman, 1965.

Kakwani, N.C.: *Income Inequality and Poverty: Methods of Estimation and Policy Applications.* Oxford: Oxford University Press, 1980.

Khader, Bichara, and Badran, Adnan (eds.): *The Economic Development of Jordan.* London: Croom Helm, 1987.

Kuznets, Simon: "Economic Growth and Income Inequality." *American Economic Review* 45 (1955), pp. 1-28.

Lecaillon, J., Paukert, F., Morrison, C., and Germidis, D.: *Income Distribution and Economic Development.* Geneva: ILO, 1984.

Leibenstein, H.: *Economic Backwardness and Economic Growth.* New York: Wiley, 1957.

Lewis, A.: "Economic Development with Unlimited Supplies of Labour." *Manchaster School Economic and Social Studies* 22 (1954), pp. 400-499.

Lewis, W.A.: *The Theory of Economic Growth.* Homewood, Ill.: Irwin, 1955.

Little, I.M.D.: *Economic Development--Theory, Policy and International Relations.* New York: Basic Book, 1982.

MacEachron, A.E.: *Basic Statistics in the Human Service.* Baltimore, Md.: University Park Press, 1982.

Malkawi, A.: *Regional Development in Jordan--Some Aspects of the Urban Bias.* Amman: Royal Scientific Society, 1978.

Mazur, M.: *Economic Growth and Development in Jordan*. London: Croom Helm, 1979.

Mehmet, O.: *Economic Planning and Social Justice in Developing Countries*. London: Croom Helm, 1978.

Metzer, J., Orth, M., and Sterzing, C.: *Das ist unser Land: West Bank and Gaza Streifen unter Israelischer Besatzung*. Bornheim-Merten, 1980.

Mikhail, W.M.: "A Standard Aggregative Model for the Jordanian Economy." *International Journal of Middle East Studies* 17 (1) (1985), pp. 67-88.

Ministry of Health, Department of Planning: *Statistical Annual Report, 1982*. Amman, n.d.

_____: *Statistical Annual Report, 1985*. Amman, n.d.

_____: *Statistical Annual Report, 1986*. Amman, n.d.

Ministry of Labor: *Labor Magazine, nos. 27-28* (1984)/(Arabic).

Ministry of Planning: *Five Year Plan for Economic and Social Development 1981-1985*. Amman, 1981.

_____: *Five Year Plan for Economic and Social Development, 1986-1990*. Amman, 1986.

Ministry of Social Development: *Pockets of Poverty in Jordan, 1987*. Forthcoming.

National Medical Enterprises: *Jordan Country and Health Profile*. NME International, n.d.

National Planning Council: *Three Year Development Plan, 1973-1975*. Amman, 1972.

_____: *Five Year Developing PLan, 1976-1980*. Amman, 1976.

Odeh, M.: "Some Effects That Accompanied Woman's Work in Jordan." *Labor Magazine*. Nos. 25-26 (1984)/(Arabic).

Paukert, F.: "Income Distribution at Different Levels of Development." *International Labour Review* (1973), pp. 97-125.

Radwan, S.: *Agrarian Reform and Rural Poverty, Egypt, 1952-1975*. Geneva: ILO, 1977.

Reynolds, L.G.: *Labour Economics and Labour Relations*. Englewood Cliffs, N.J.: Prentice-Hall, 1978.

Robert, B. at al: *A History of Economic Theory and Methods*. New York: McGraw-Hill, 1975.

Roy, Sara: *The Gaza Strip Survey*. Jerusalem: West Bank Data Base Project, 1986.

Royal Scientific Society, Economic Research Department: *Demand Analysis in Jordan*. Amman: Royal Scientific Society, 1985.

Saket, Bassam K., Al-Tell, Tariq, Zreigat, Sami, and Asfour, Bassam: *Workers Migration Abroad: Socio-Economic Implications for Households in Jordan*. Amman: Royal Scientific Society, 1983.

Sen, A.: "On the Development of Basic Income Indicators to Supplement GNP Measures." *Economic Bulletin for Asia and Far East (U.N.)* 24 (1983).

_____: *Poverty and Famines: An Essay on Entitlement and Deprivation*. Oxford: Oxford University Press, 1984.

Sha'ban, R.A.: *Expenditure Distribution and Poverty in Jordan*. Philadelphia: University of Pennsylvania, June 1987, unpublished.

_____: *The Distribution of Economic Welfare in Jordan*. Forthcoming.

Shultz, T.W.: "Value of the Children." *Journal of Political Economy* 81 (2)

(Supplement, 1973), p. 13.

Sloane, P.J.: "The Structure of Labour Market and Low Pay for Women." In Sloane, P.J. (ed.): *Women and Low Pay*. London: Macmillan, 1980.

Smadi, M.A., Amerah, M.S., Ali, M.I.T., El-Ahmad, A.Q., and Al Yousef, F.S.: *The Socio-Economic Impact of Guest Workers in Jordan*. Amman: Royal Scientific Society, 1986.

Smadi, Mohammad, Ali, M.I.T., Amerah, M.S., and Ibrahim, I.J.: *The Unemployment Problem in Jordan: Characteristics and Prospects*. Amman: Royal Scientific Society, November 1987.

Standing, G.: *Labour Force Participation and Economic Development*. Geneva: ILO, 1978.

Tarawneh, F.: "Income Inequality and Poverty in Mexico: Quantitative Assessments and Explanations." Ph.D. diss., University of Southern California, 1980.

_____: "Poverty and the Distribution of Growth in Jordan." *Banks of Jordan Magazine* 3 (1983).

Taylor, Lance, and Arida, Persio: "Long-Run Income Distribution and Growth." In Chenery, H., and Srinivasan, T.N. (eds.): *Handbook of Development Economics, 1*. Amsterdam: North-Holland, 1988, pp. 161-194.

Touqan, S., and Al-Shunnaq, M.: "Report to the 'Pockets of Poverty in Jordan' Study Project." Amman: 1987, unpublished.

Turner, H.A.: "Inflation and Wage Differentials in Great Britain." In Dunlop, J.T. (ed.): *The Theory of Wage Discrimination*. London: Macmillian, 1955.

United Nation Children's Fund/Ministry of Health: *Situation Analysis: Children and Women in the Hashemite Kingdom of Jordan*. Amman: 1989, unpublished.

United Nation Relief and Work Agency for Palestine Refugees in the Near East, Department of Information: *UNWRA Publications*. Amman: UNWRA, January 1987.

United States Department of Agriculture: *Survey, 1977-1978*. Washington, D.C.: United States Government Printing Office, 1979.

Van Ginnecken, W.: *Characteristics of the Head of the Household and Income Inequality: Mexico*. Geneva: ILO, 1975.

Vocational Training Corporation: *Training and Job Opportunities for Women in Jordan*. Amman, December 1981.

Weintraub, R.: "The Birth Rate and Economic Development: An Empirical Study." *Econometrica* 30 (4) (1962), pp. 812-817.

Weiss, D.: "Ueberlegungen zur Jordanischen Entwicklungsplanung." *Konjunkturpolitik* 29 (1) (1983),

World Bank: *Jordan--Efficiency and Equity of Government Revenues and Social Expenditures*. 2 Vols. Washington, D.C: World Bank, Report no. 5697-Jo., July 1985, unpublished.

_____: *World Bank Development Report, 1985*. New York: Oxford University Press, 1985.

_____: *Jordan: Issues of Employment and Labour Market Imbalances*. 2 Vols. Washington, D.C.: World Bank, Report no. 5117-Jo., 1986.

_____: *World Bank Development Report, 1988*. New York: Oxford University Press, 1988.

Zahlan, A.B. (ed.): *The Agriculture Sector of Jordan: Policy and System Studies.* London: Ithaca Press, 1985.

About the Editors and Authors

Kamel Abu Jaber, born 1932, Ph.D. in political science, Syracuse University, United States: 1965, assistant professor, University of Tennessee; 1967, associate professor, Smith College; 1971, full professor, University of Jordan; 1973, minister of national economy of the Hashemite Kingdom of Jordan; various assignments at the University of Jordan as dean of faculty and director of centers.

Abdelfattah Abu Shokor, born 1949, Dr. Phil. in political economics from Phillips University, Marburg, Federal Republic of Germany: at present associate professor of economics at An-Najah National University, Nablus, Palestine; since 1984, dean of faculty of economics and administrative sciences at An-Najah National University. Current research interests include macroeconomic theory and economic and labor development in West Bank and Gaza Strip. Many publications in these fields of research.

Matthes Buhbe, born 1949, Dr. Rer. Pol. in political economics from the University of Dortmund, Federal Republic of Germany: held teaching and research assignments at the Universities of Regensburg and Dortmund before joining the research institute of Friedrich Ebert Stiftung (FES), Bonn, Federal Republic of Germany; since 1986, resident representative of FES in Amman, Jordan.

Adeeb Haddad, born 1942, Dr. in econometrics from Oklahoma State University, United States: held teaching and research assignments at the various Jordanian universities and academic institutions; currently employed by the Central Bank of Jordan as an executive director of the department of research and studies; board of director member in numerous Jordanian financial institutions; academic dean of Banking Studies Institute.

Taher H. Kana'an, born 1935, Ph.D. in economics from Cambridge University, United Kingdom: since 1986, Jordanian minister of planning; ex-minister of Occupied Territories affairs (1985-1986); held a number of executive and advisory positions with United Nations and pan-Arab organisations; served as the chief economist in a major industrial consultancy for the Morrocan Ministry of Planning and as economic adviser at the Iraqi Ministry of Planning; board member of the Arab Unity Studies Center and a member of the Arab Thought Forum, Arab Association for Economic Research, and Arab Society for Human Rights. Papers and publications are in the areas of input-output analysis and development issues of Third World countries.

Abed Kharabsheh, born 1949, Ph. D. in economics and statistics from University of Missouri, Columbia, United States: at present, assistant professor of economics and statistics at the University of Jordan; after graduation, joined the Central Bank of Jordan; was a graduate assistant at the University of Jordan.

Saleh Al-Khasawneh, born 1940, Ph.D. and DBA (major: economics; minor: statistics and MKT) from Texas University, United States: after graduation, joined the University of Jordan where he worked as assistant, associate professor, chair for the economics department, and then director general for the department of planning and development; in 1977, joined the civil service, where he was director general of income tax department (1977-1981); economic chancellor for the prime minister (1981-1984); and secretary general for the minister of labor (1984-present); board member and chair of directors of various national institutions and establishments.

Ahmad Malkawi, born 1941, Dr. in economics from the High School of Economics, Prague, Czechoslovakia: since 1984, director of planning and statistics, University of Jordan; joined the department of economics and statistics of the University of Jordan in 1981; before served as economic researcher at the Royal Scientific Society, Amman.

Ghassan Musallam, born 1949, Doctorat D'Etat in economics from the Université de Bordeaux, France: held research assignments (financial and human resources) at the Council for Arab Economic Unity in 1970-1980; joined Social Security Corporation in late 1980 and now is the director of its investment department.

Mohammad Al-Saqour, born 1936, Dr. in social and regional planning from Almenia University, Egypt: worked with government of Jordan and as U.N. expert in various social fields before joining in 1987 the Ministry of Social Development of Jordan; assignment as undersecretary of state for social development.

Radwan Ali Sha'ban, born 1957, Ph.D. in economics from Stanford University, United States: consultant to Jordan's Ministry of Planning and assistant professor of economics at the University of Pennsylvania, United States; visited Kuwait Institute for Scientific Research during 1988-1989.

Mohammad Smadi, born 1950, Ph.D. in economics from University of Keele, United Kingdom: held various positions at the Royal Scientific Society, Amman; since 1984, director of economics research department at the society; membership in a number of governmental committees and expert missions abroad.

Fayez A. Tarawneh, born 1949, Ph.D. in economics from University of Southern California, United States: after graduation, joined the Royal Service; assistant chief of the Royal Protocol (1971-1980); in 1980, joined the civil service, where he worked as economic secretary to the prime minister (1980-1984); economic adviser to the prime minister (1984-1988); and minister of state for prime ministry affairs (1988); at present, he is minister of supply.